New Mexico Dreamscapes

Bobby J. Jones

Copyright © 2018   Bobby J. Jones

All rights reserved.

ISBN: 1986596095
ISBN-13: 9781986596091

DEDICATION

I dedicate New Mexico Dreamscapes and its images to the loving memory of my mother Kate Brown Jones.

Table of Contents

KNOWLEDGMENT	**Page 8**
Image 1	Page 10
Image 2	Page 12
Image 3	Page 14
Image 4	Page 16
Image 5	Page 18
Image 6	Page 20
Image 7	Page 22
Image 8	Page 24
Image 9	**Page 26**
Image 10	Page 28
Image 11	Page 30
Image 12	Page 32
Image 13	Page 34
Image 14	Page 36
Image 15	Page 38
Image 16	Page 40
Image 17	Page 42
Image 18	Page 44
Image 19	Page 46
Image 20	Page 48
Image 21	Page 50
Image 22	Page 52
Image 23	Page 54
Image 24	Page 56

Image 25	Page 58
Image 26	Page 60
Image 27	Page 62
Image 28	Page 64
Image 29	Page 66
Image 30	Page 68
Image 31	Page 70
Image 32	Page 72
Image 33	Page 74
Image 34	Page 76
Image 35	Page 78
Image 36	Page 80
Image 37	Page 82
Image 38	Page 84
Image 39	Page 86
Image 40	Page 88
Image 41	Page 90
Image 42	Page 92
Image 43	Page 94
Image 44	Page 96
Image 45	Page 98
Image 46	Page 100
Image 47	Page 102
Image 48	Page 104
Image 49	Page 106
Image 50	Page 108
Image 51	Page 110

Image 52	Page 112
Image 53	Page 114
Image 54	Page 116
Image 55	Page 118
Image 56	Page 120
Image 57	Page 122
Image 58	Page 124
Image 59	Page 126
Image 60	Page 128
About The Author	Page 130

New Mexico Dreamscapes

ACKNOWLEDGMENTS

I would like to acknowledge my mother Kate Brown Jones for encouraging me to create art since the age of 2. As the story goes, one day my mother caught me scribbling on the linoleum tile floor in the family room to the house where I grew up in Fort Worth, Texas. My mother did not scold me. Instead, she encouragingly said to me, "Here, Bobby, are some blank sheets of paper. Keep drawing!" She lovingly placed them in front of me.

At the age of five, I was drawing pictures of houses. I fondly recall drawing two story houses that shown their interior views. I drew the furniture, appliances, etc. I drew what the inside of a house looked like to a five year old with an active imagination. I remember fondly those pictures from my childhood.

Throughout my education in The Fort Worth Independent School District, I started taking art classes my fourth grade year with Mary Ann Ward at J.T. Stevens Elementary School. I always took art classes at the schools that I attended in Fort Worth, Texas. I also found that I enjoyed taking drafting classes in middle school and high school.

When I took drafting from Harold Rogers at Southwest High School in Fort Worth, Texas, I developed a love for architectural drafting. My artistic talents flew with flying colors. I wish that I had continued taking more drafting courses from this high school teacher. He was very impressed with my drawing skills.

After graduating from Southwest High School with honors, I attended Texas Tech University (my family's alma mater) in Lubbock, Texas. I majored in Art (Painting and Drawing). I studied art under Ken Dixon, Sara Waters, Vern Funk, Paul Hanna, Hugh Gibbons, and Bill Bagley. I loved taking art history courses from Nancy Reed, Edna Glenn, Rick Dingus, and Kim Smith. I graduated from Texas Tech University with honors in 1989.

I attended The University of New Mexico in Albuquerque, NM for graduate school. I received my Masters of Art in Art Education (Museum Education, Ceramics, and Photography). I studied art education and art under David Nateman, Phil Peterson, Gustave Ntiforo, Lin Johnson, and Walt Pinto. I graduated from The University of New Mexico in 1994.

During that time, my mother contracted breast cancer for the third time. This time it spread to her spine when her doctor found the cancer. My mother passed from this illness in 1992 at the age of 57. I was 25. I recall my last visit with my family and my mother in Fort Worth, Texas before she died. My mother and I had a private conversation in her bedroom. She told me directly," Bobby, I do not want you dropping out of graduate school after I am gone. I want you to continue with your studies and earn that degree." Two years later, I honored her wishes.

Whenever I place a blank sheet of paper or blank canvas in front of me, I am acknowledging the loving memory of my mother for giving me the gift of creativity so many years ago as a child. This coloring book for children of all ages is a tribute to her. I love you and miss you very much. You are with me in spirit.

Bobby J. Jones

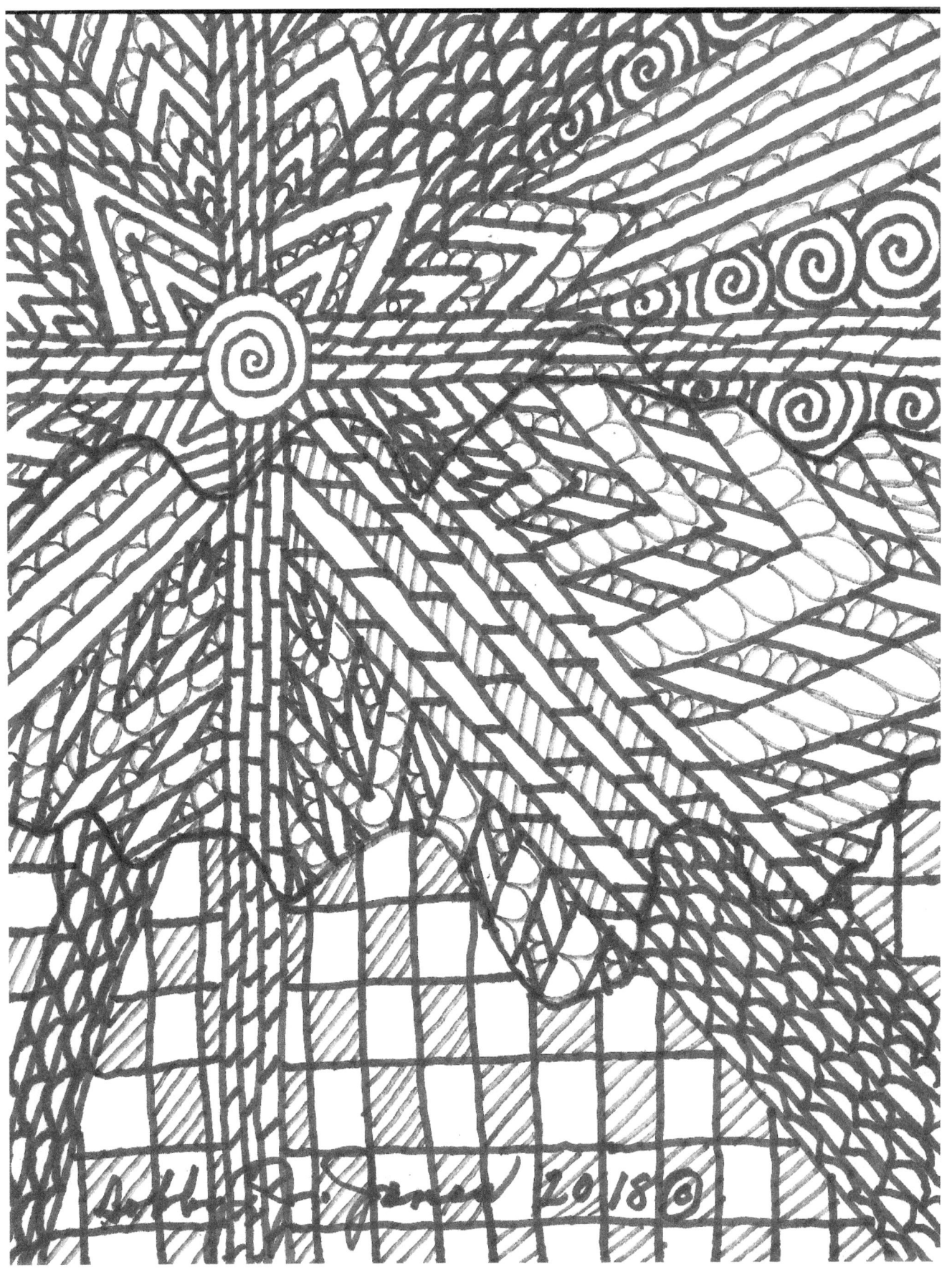

New Mexico Dreamscapes

Bobby J. Jones

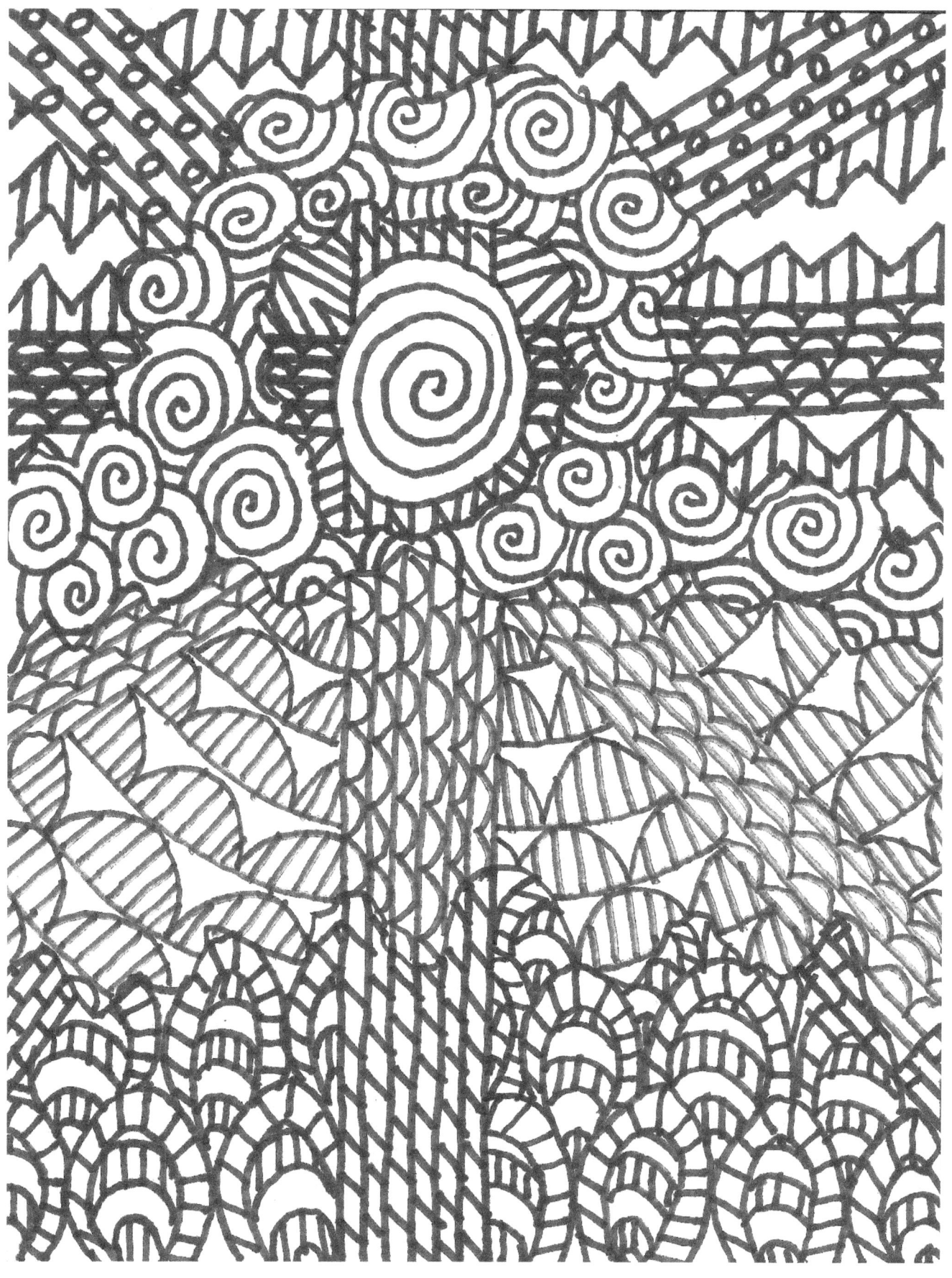

New Mexico Dreamscapes

Bobby J. Jones

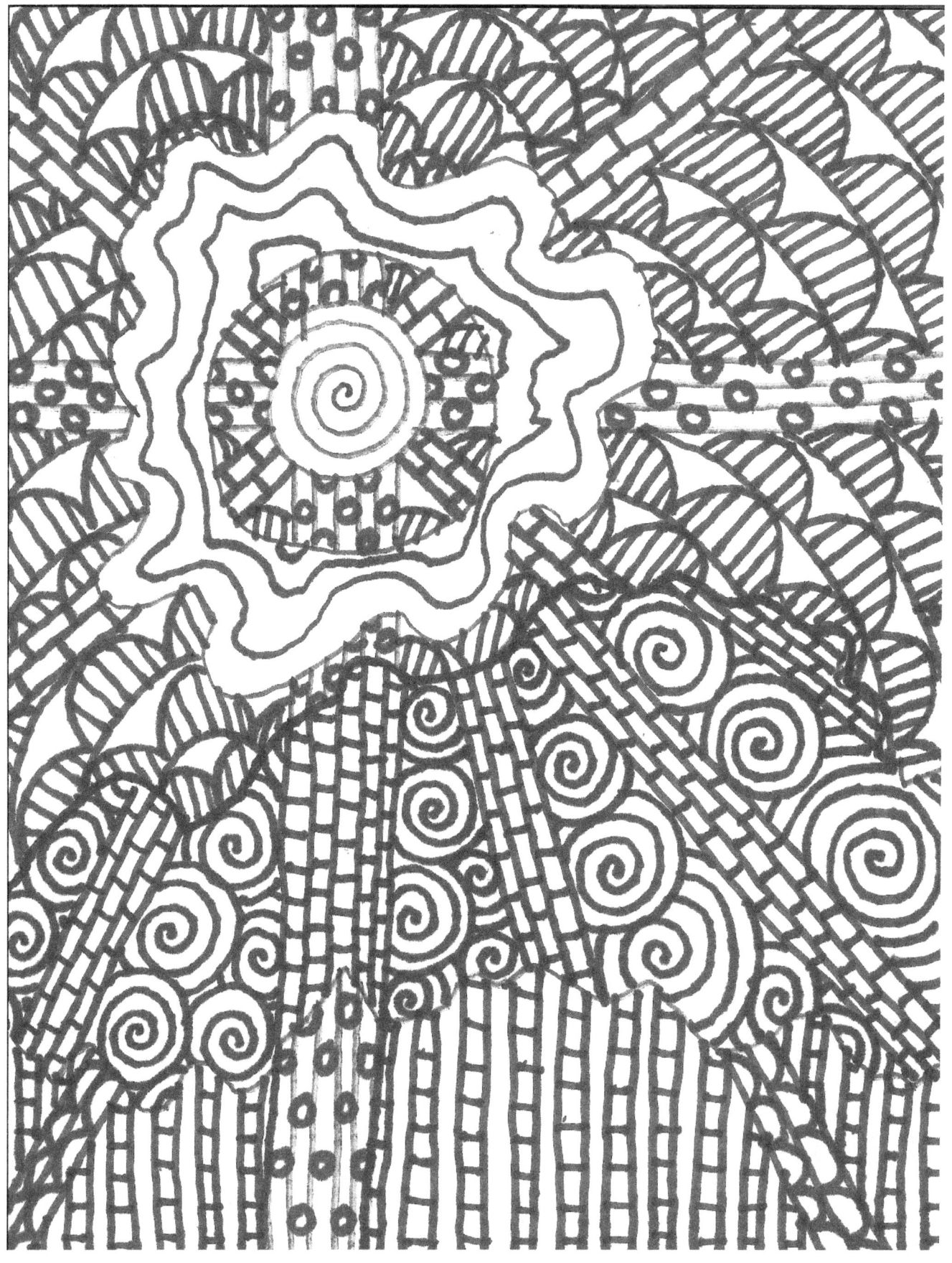

New Mexico Dreamscapes

Bobby J. Jones

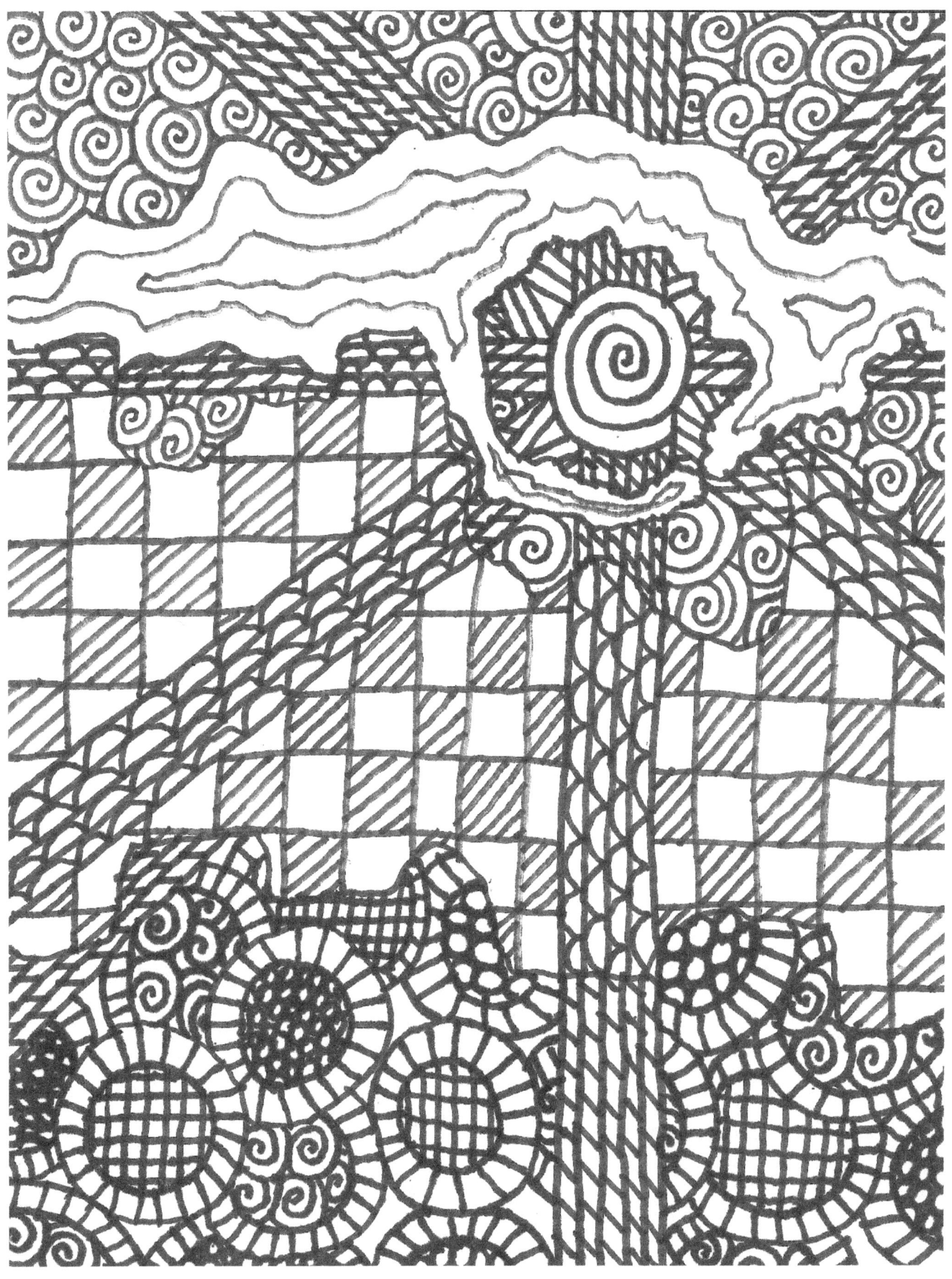

New Mexico Dreamscapes

New Mexico Dreamscapes

Bobby J. Jones

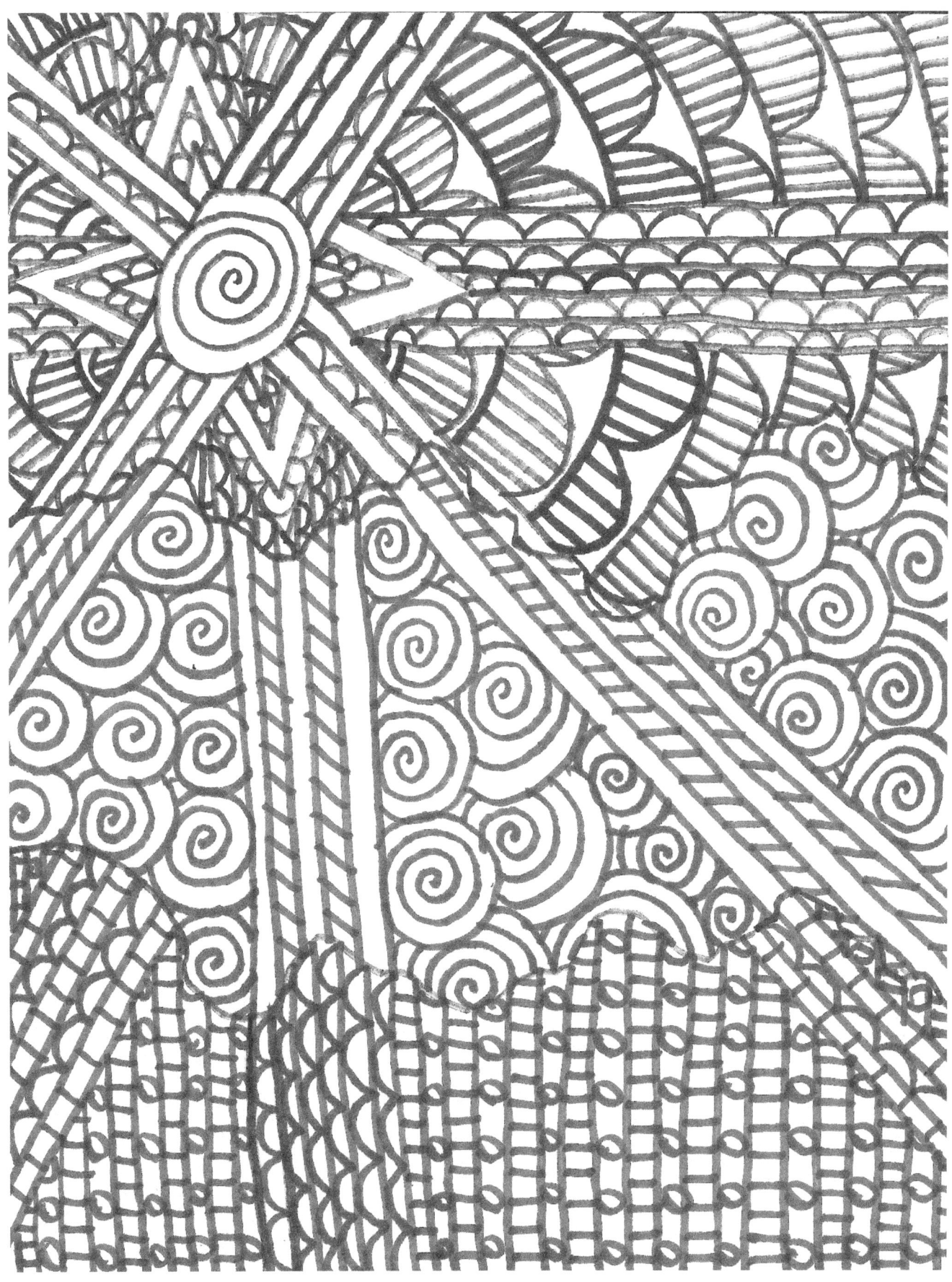

New Mexico Dreamscapes

Bobby J. Jones

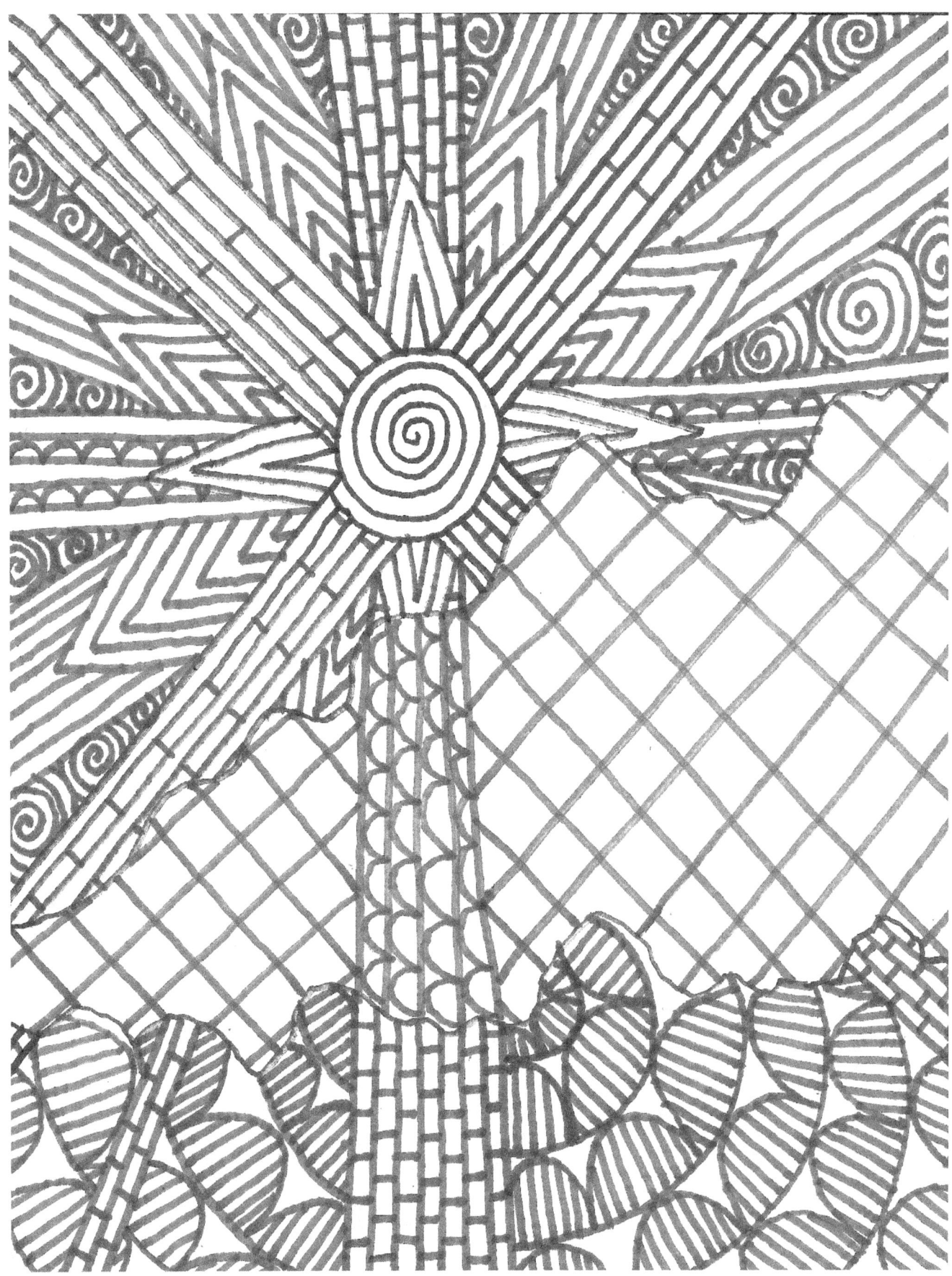

New Mexico Dreamscapes

Bobby J. Jones

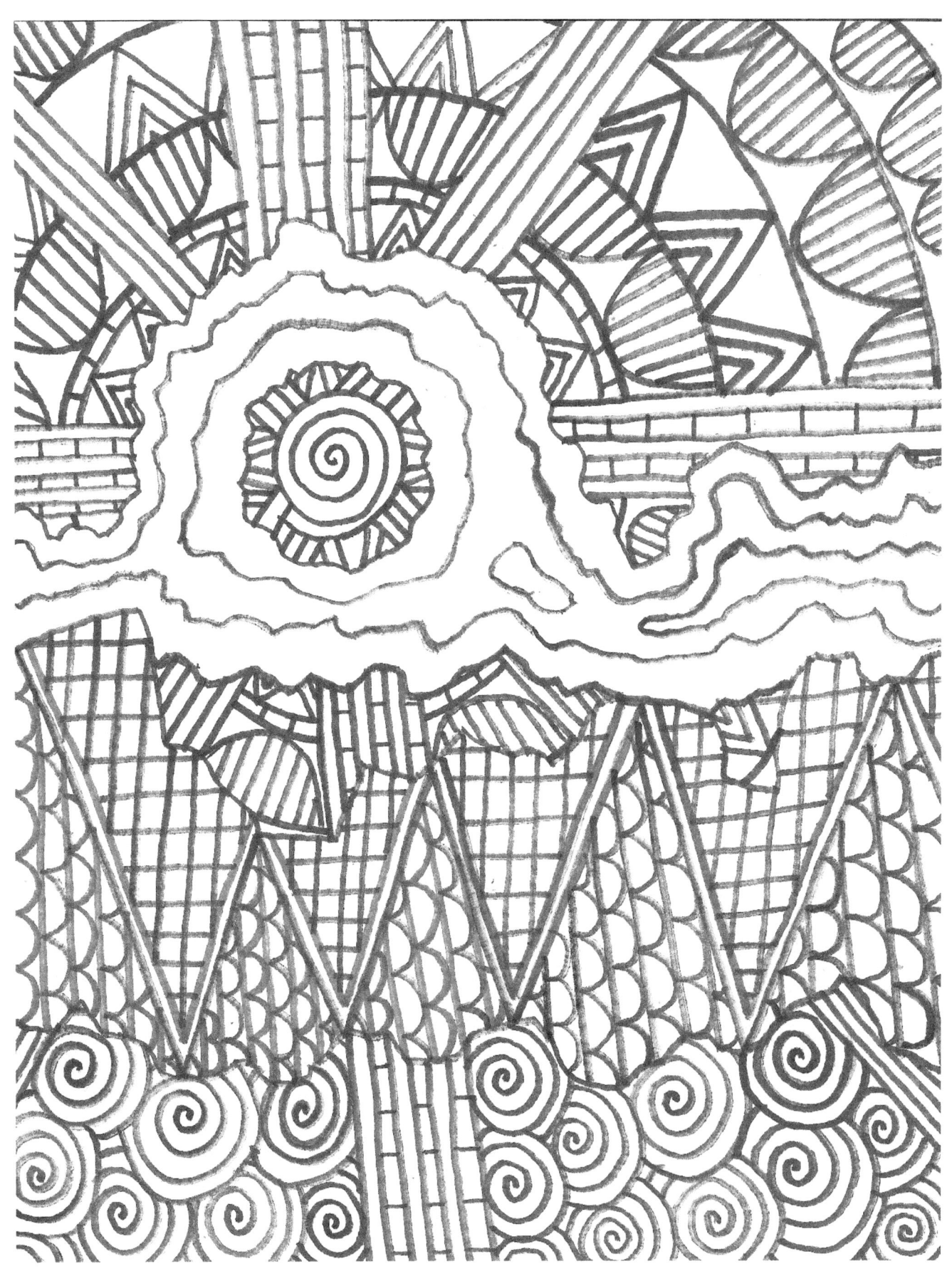

New Mexico Dreamscapes

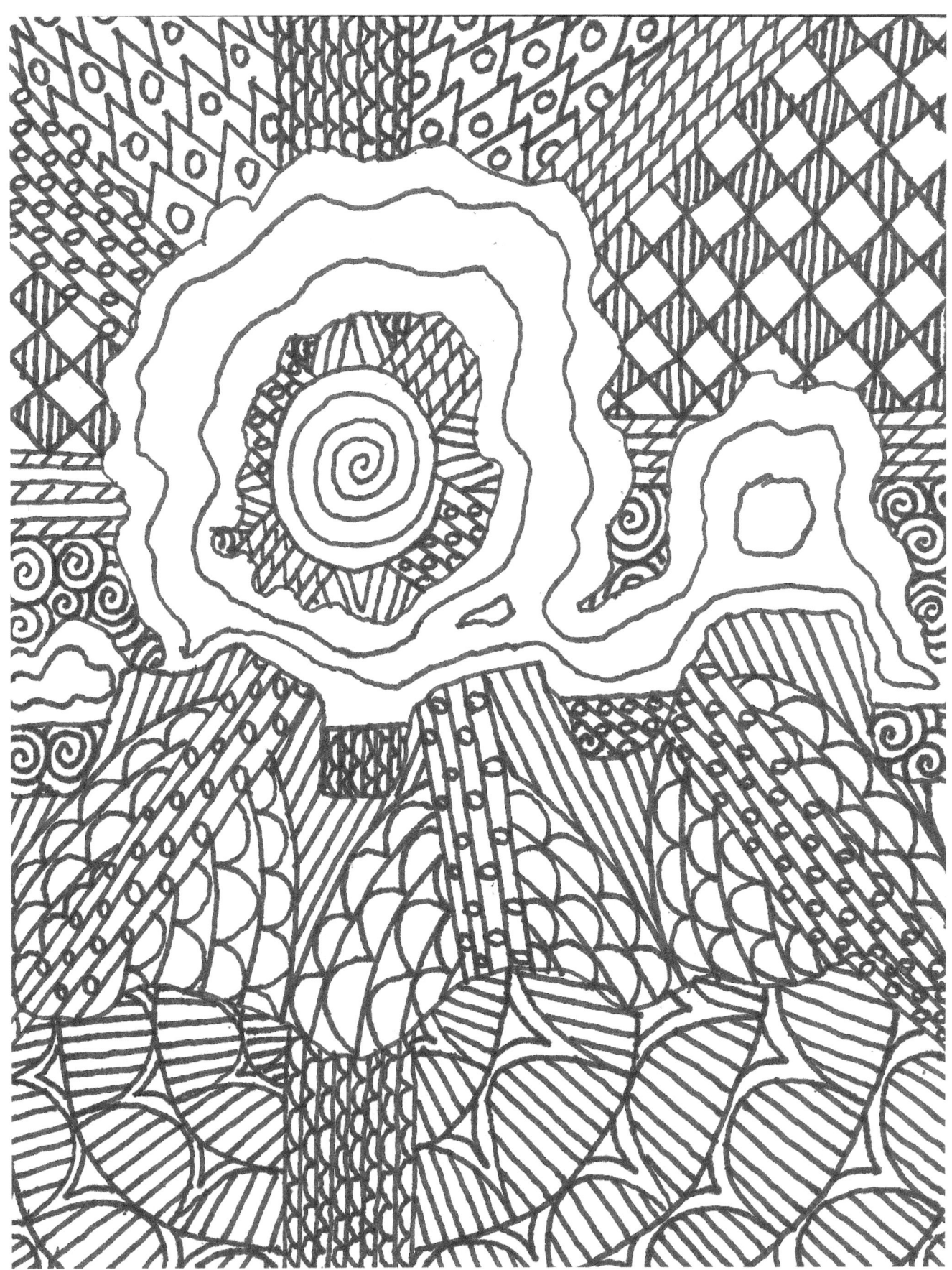

New Mexico Dreamscapes

Bobby J. Jones

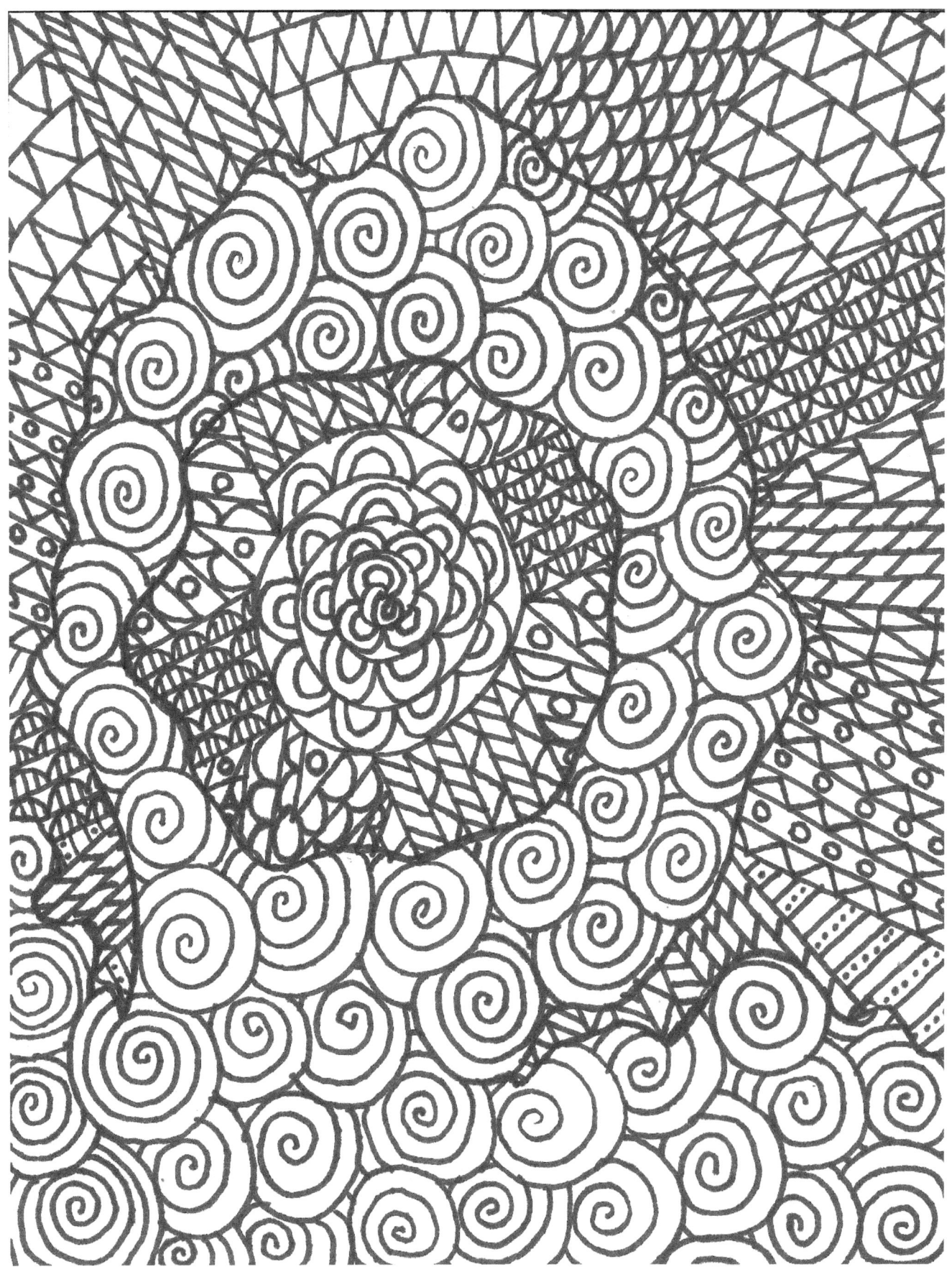

Bobby J. Jones

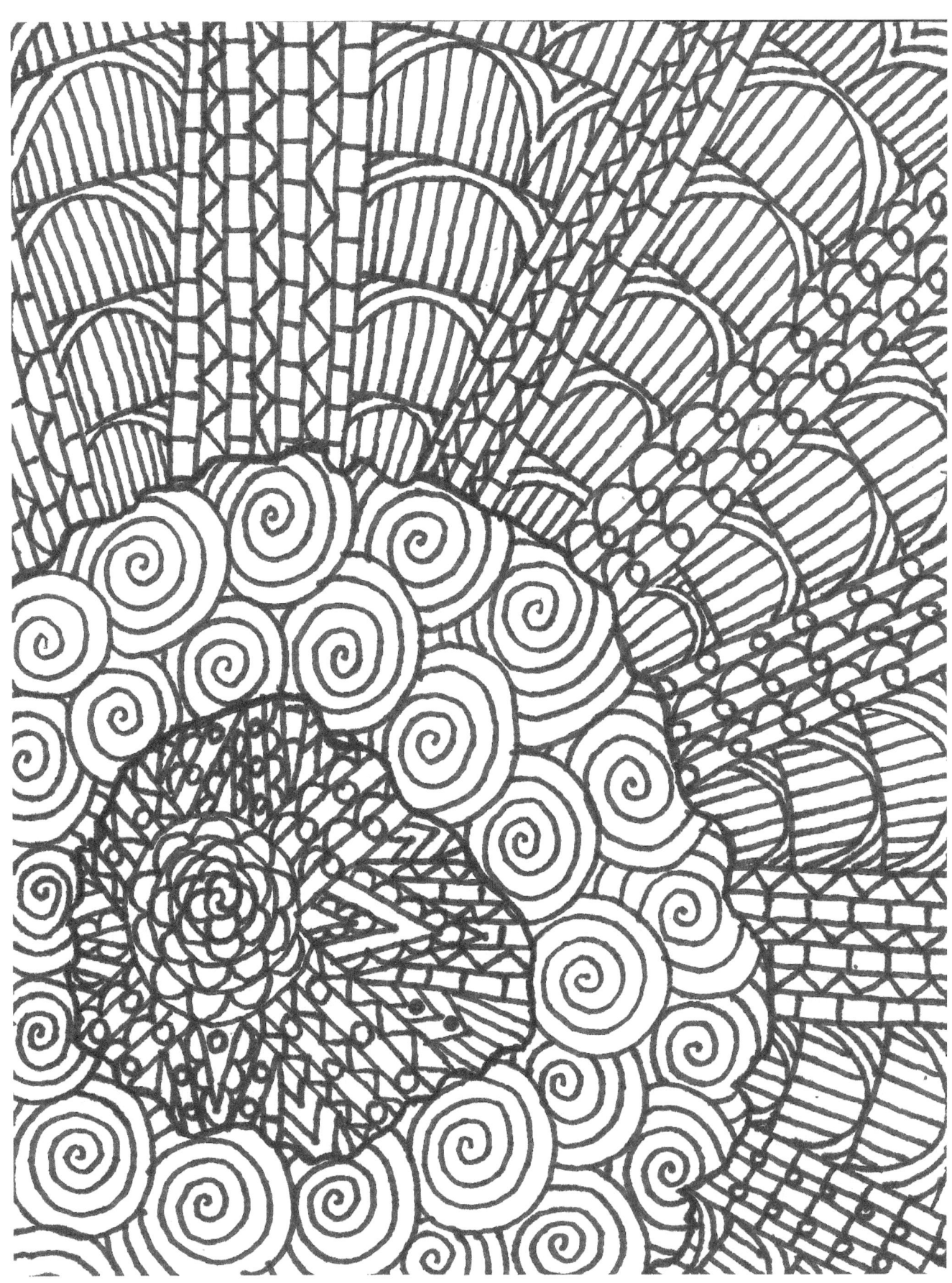

New Mexico Dreamscapes

Bobby J. Jones

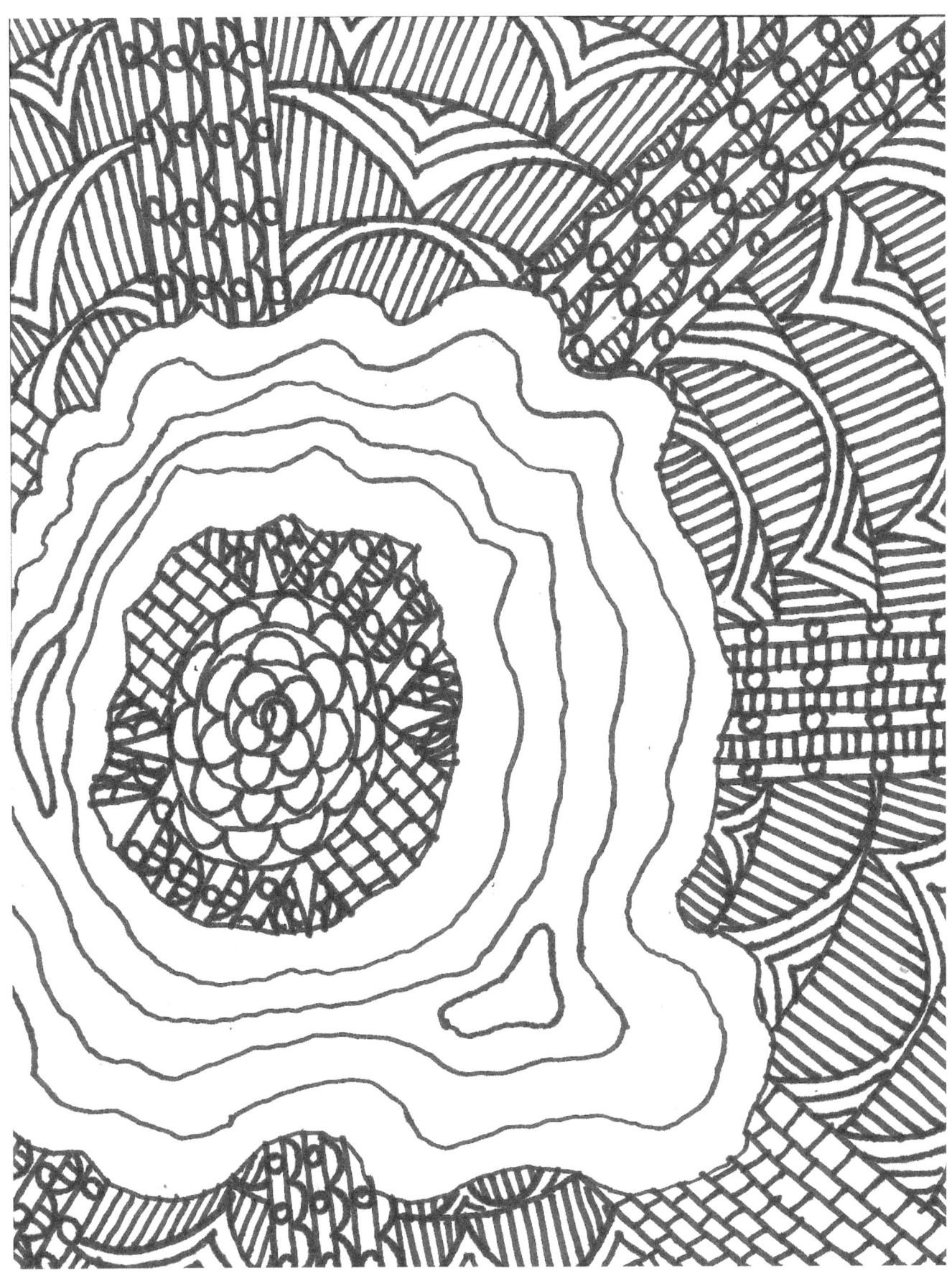

New Mexico Dreamscapes

Bobby J. Jones

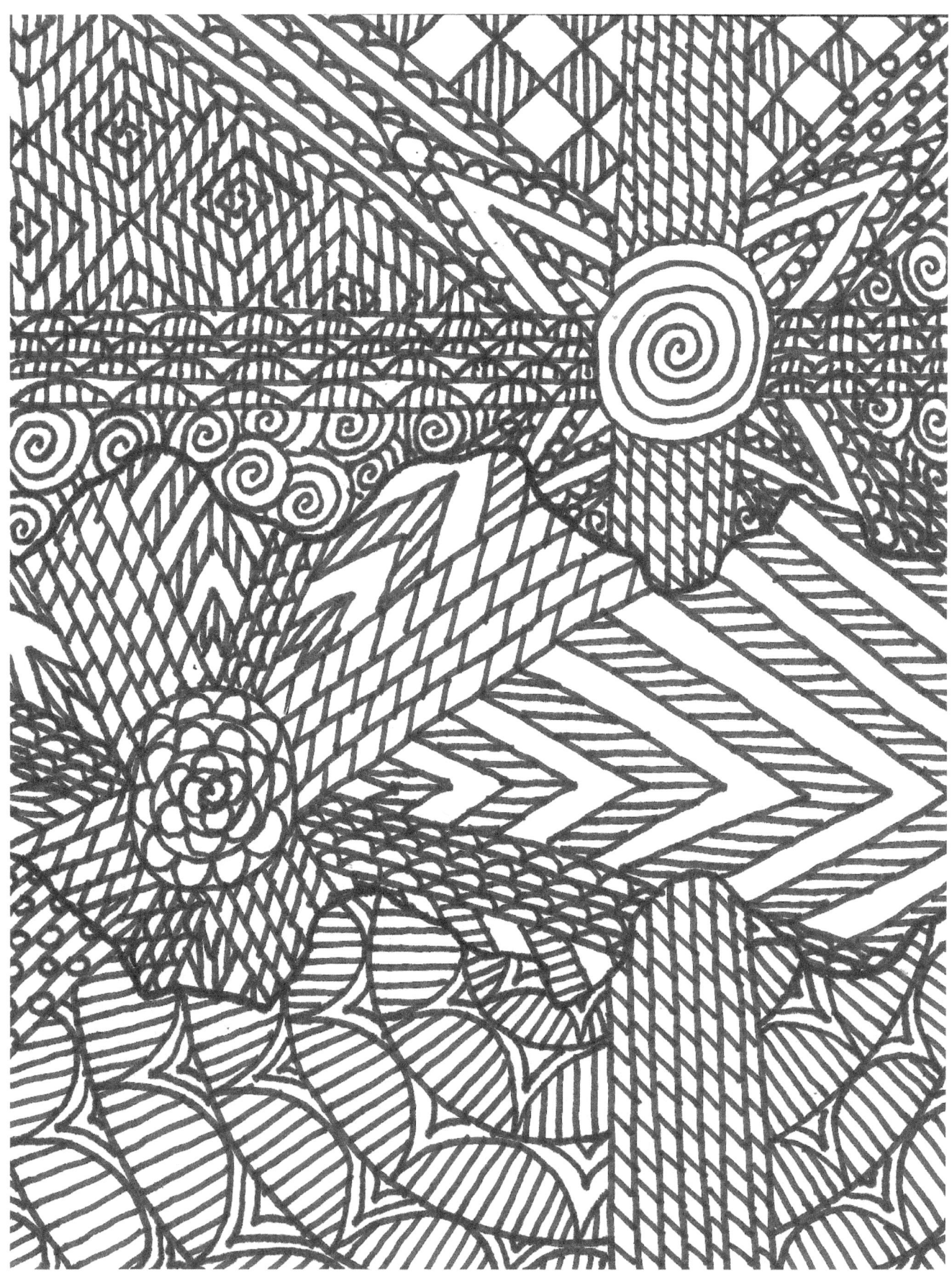

New Mexico Dreamscapes

Bobby J. Jones

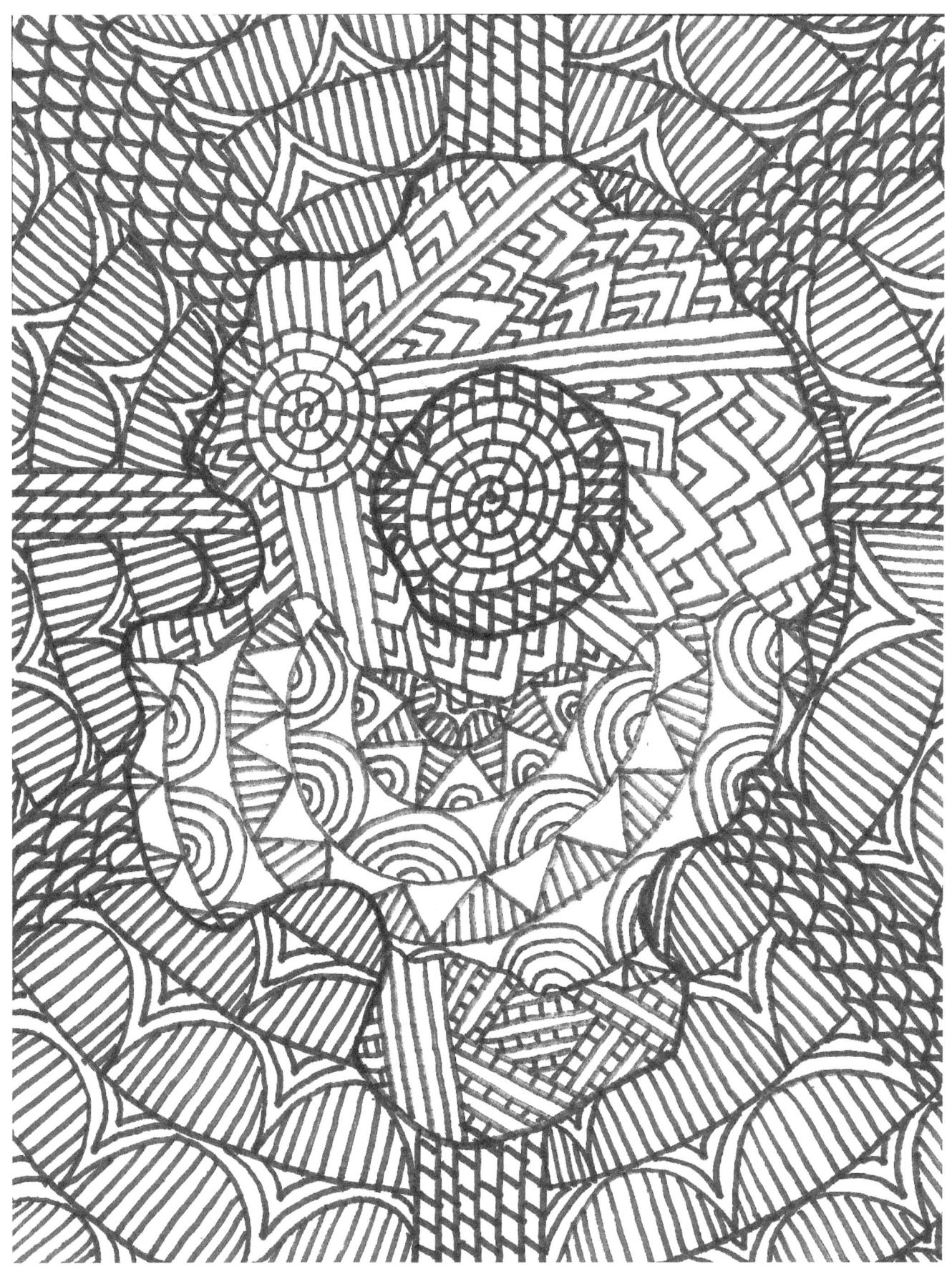

Bobby J. Jones

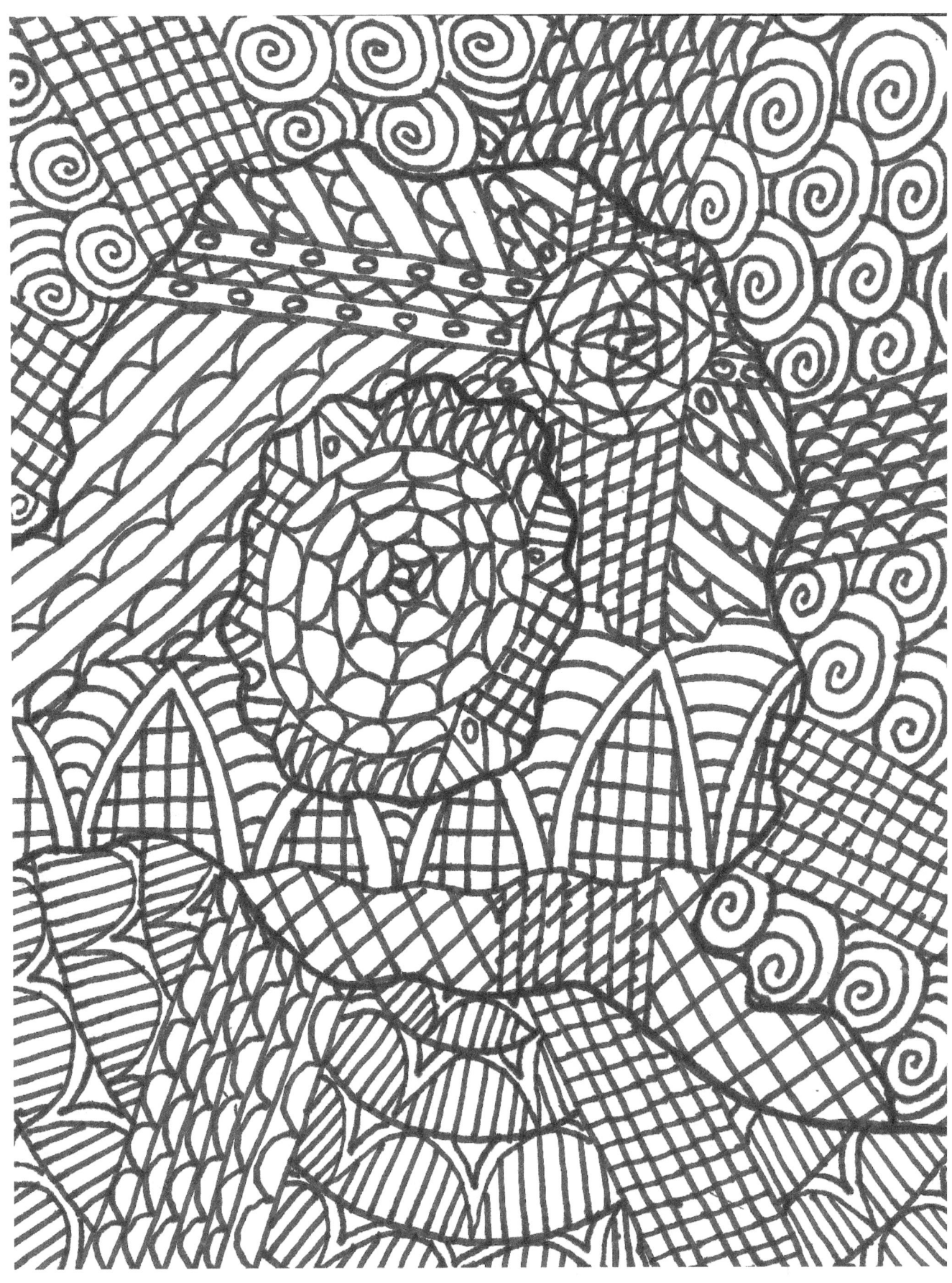

New Mexico Dreamscapes

Bobby J. Jones

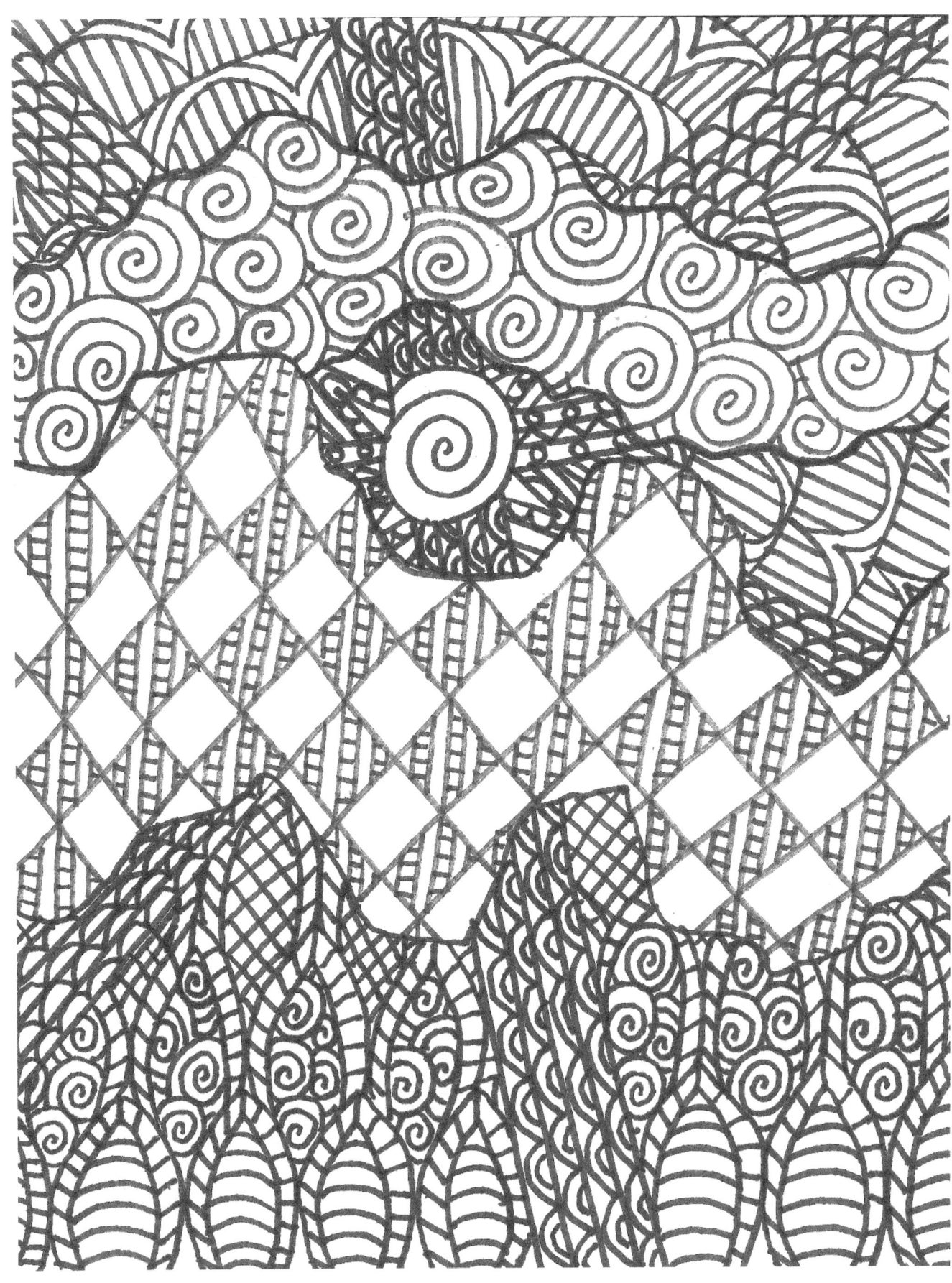

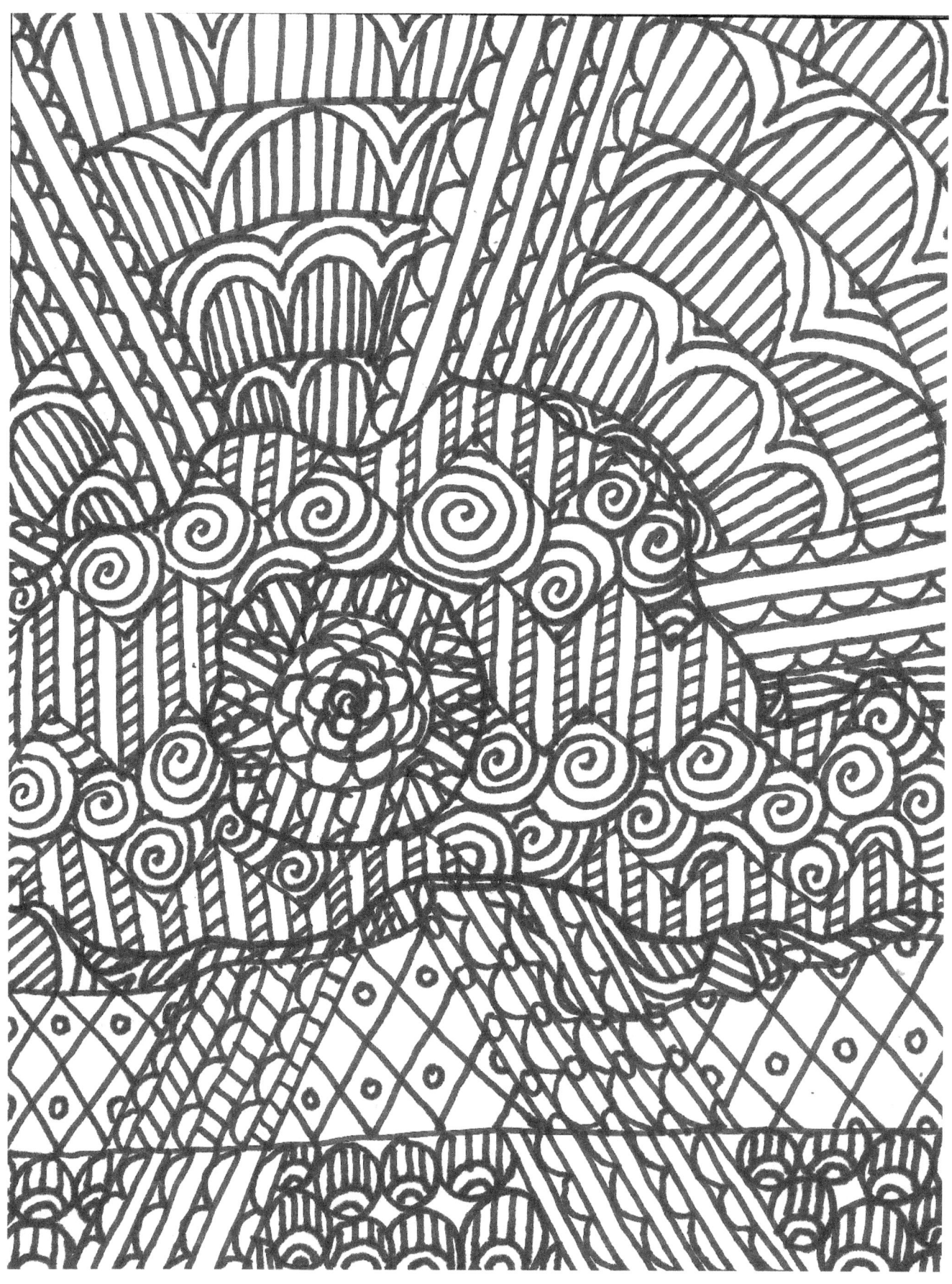

Bobby J. Jones

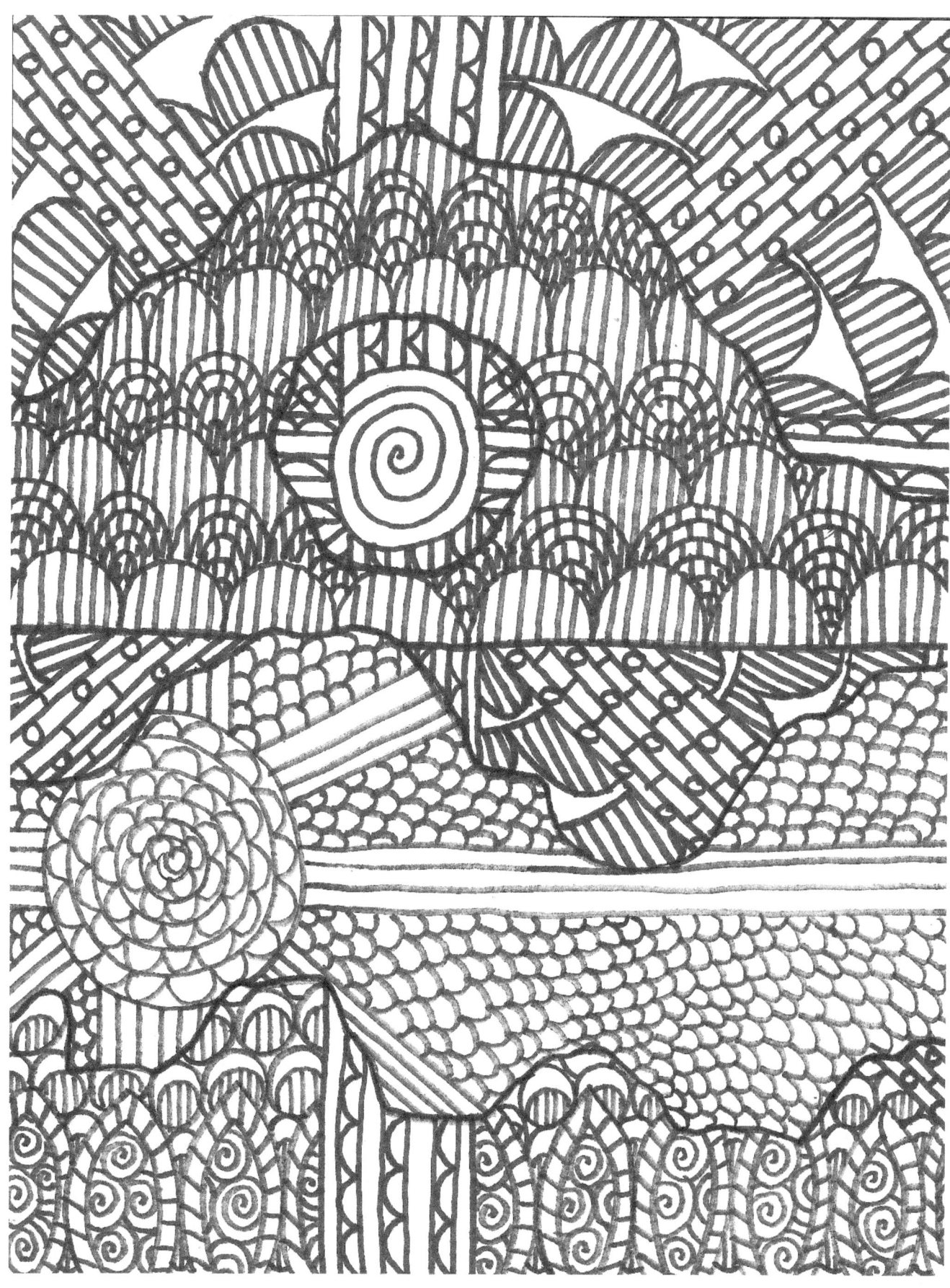

Bobby J. Jones

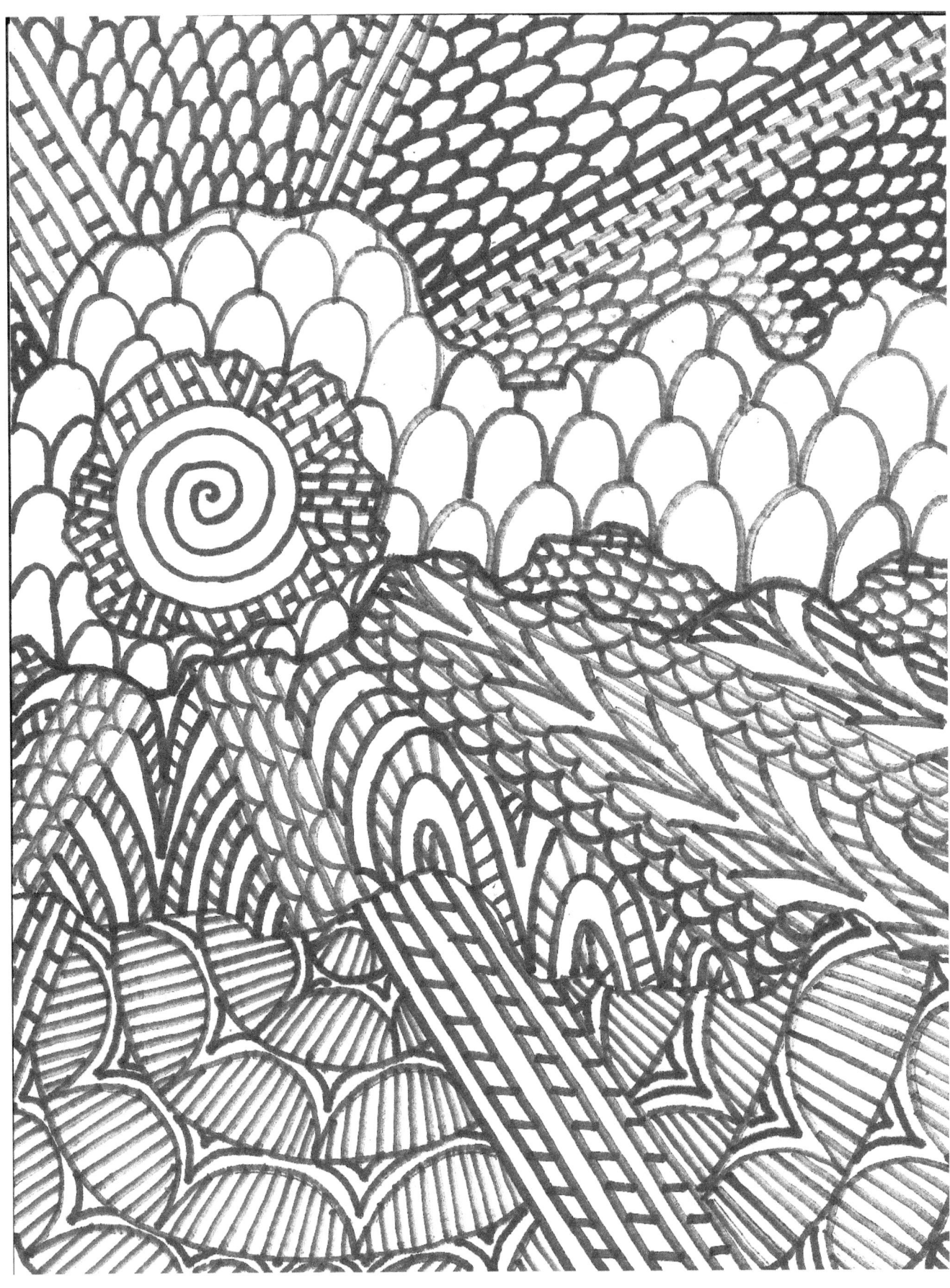

New Mexico Dreamscapes

Bobby J. Jones

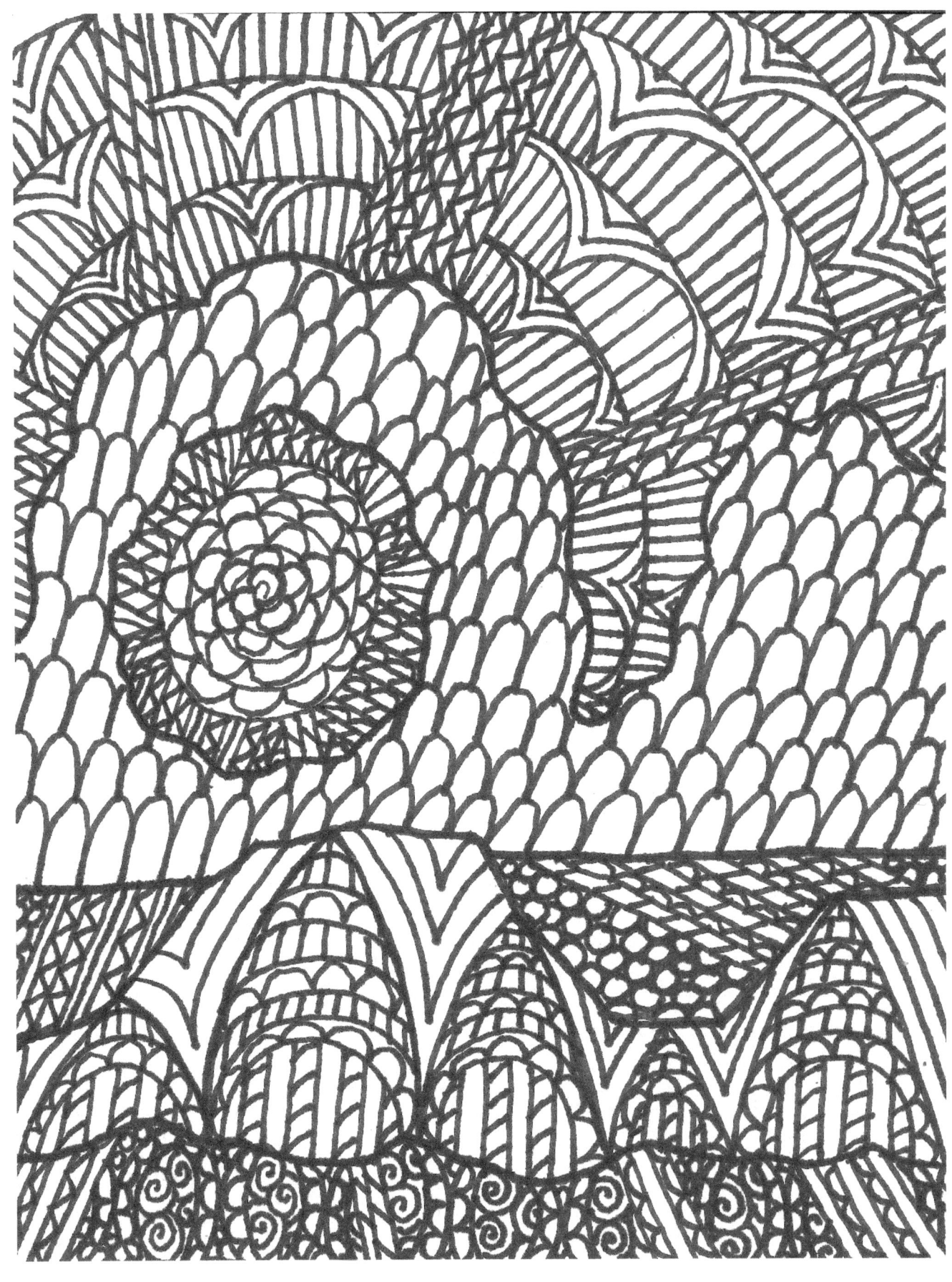

Bobby J. Jones

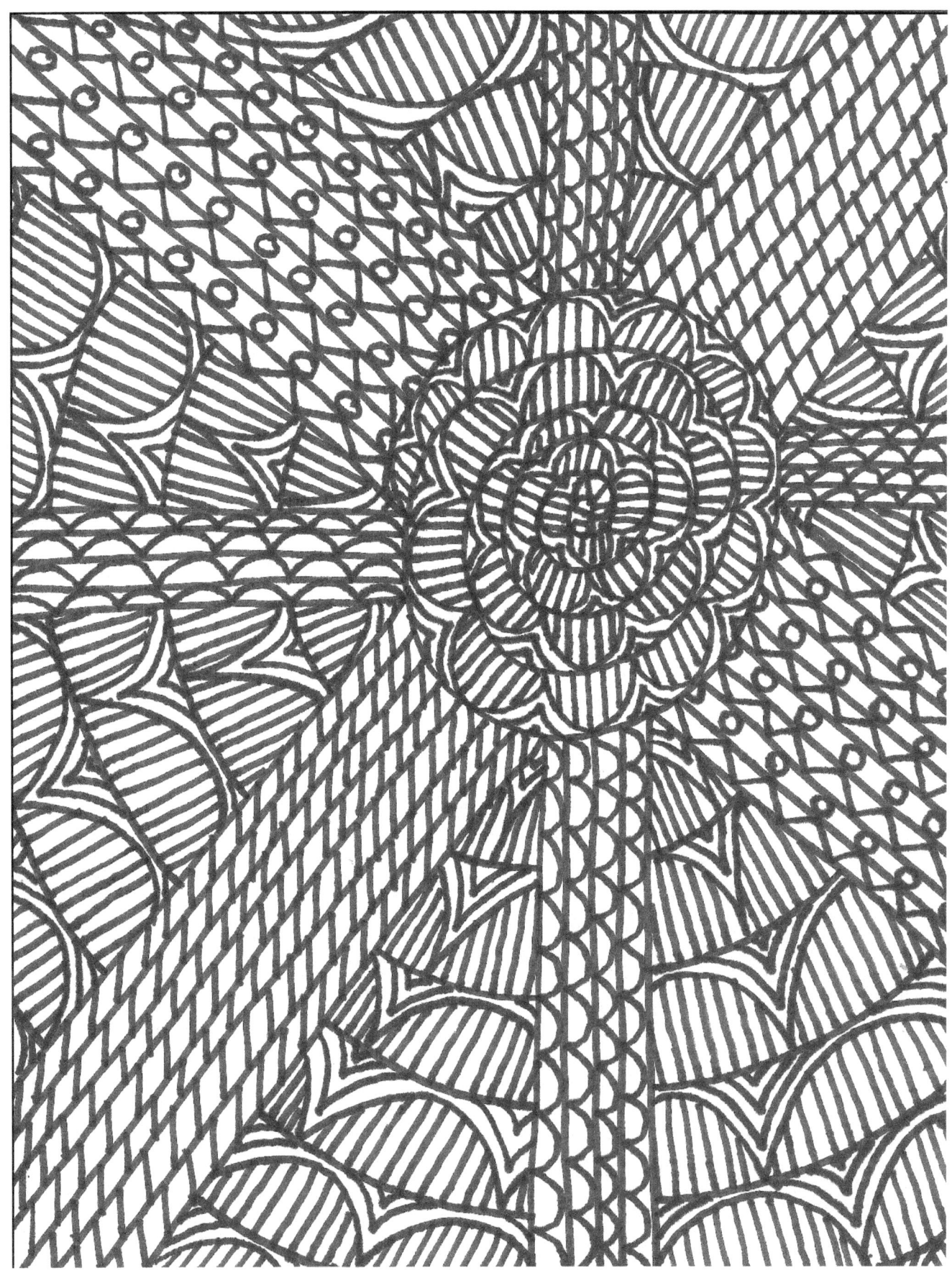

New Mexico Dreamscapes

Bobby J. Jones

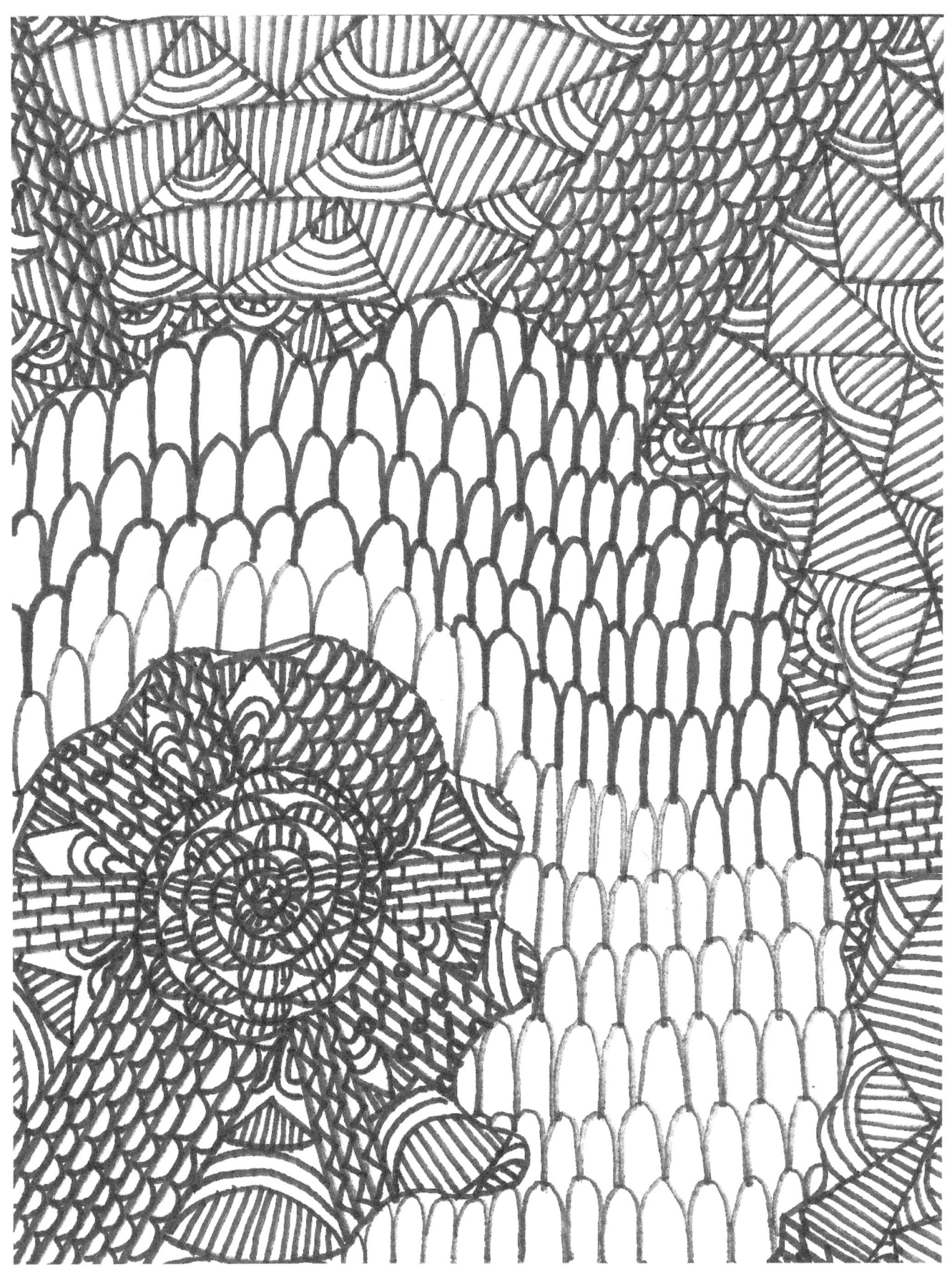

New Mexico Dreamscapes

Bobby J. Jones

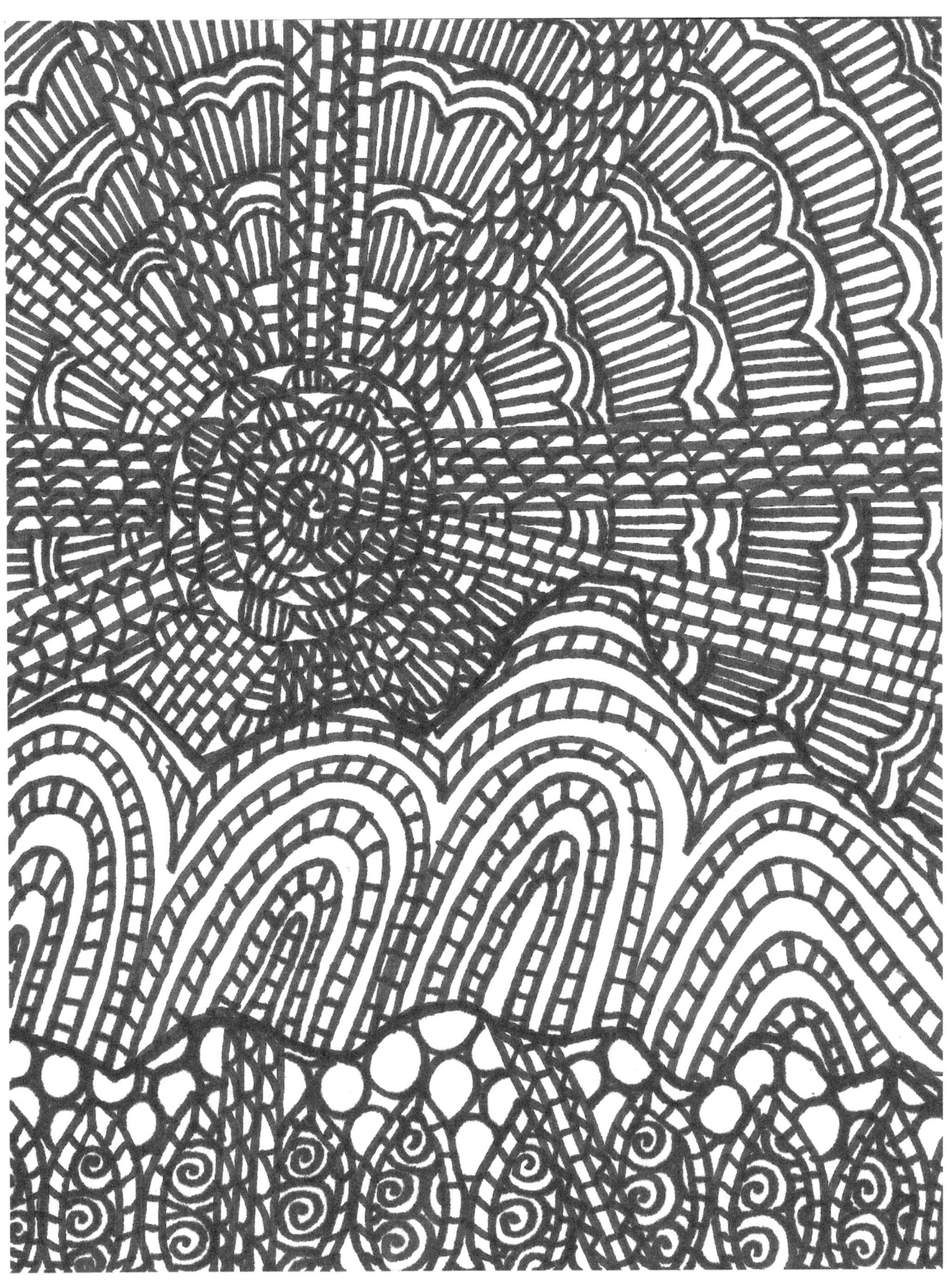

New Mexico Dreamscapes

Bobby J. Jones

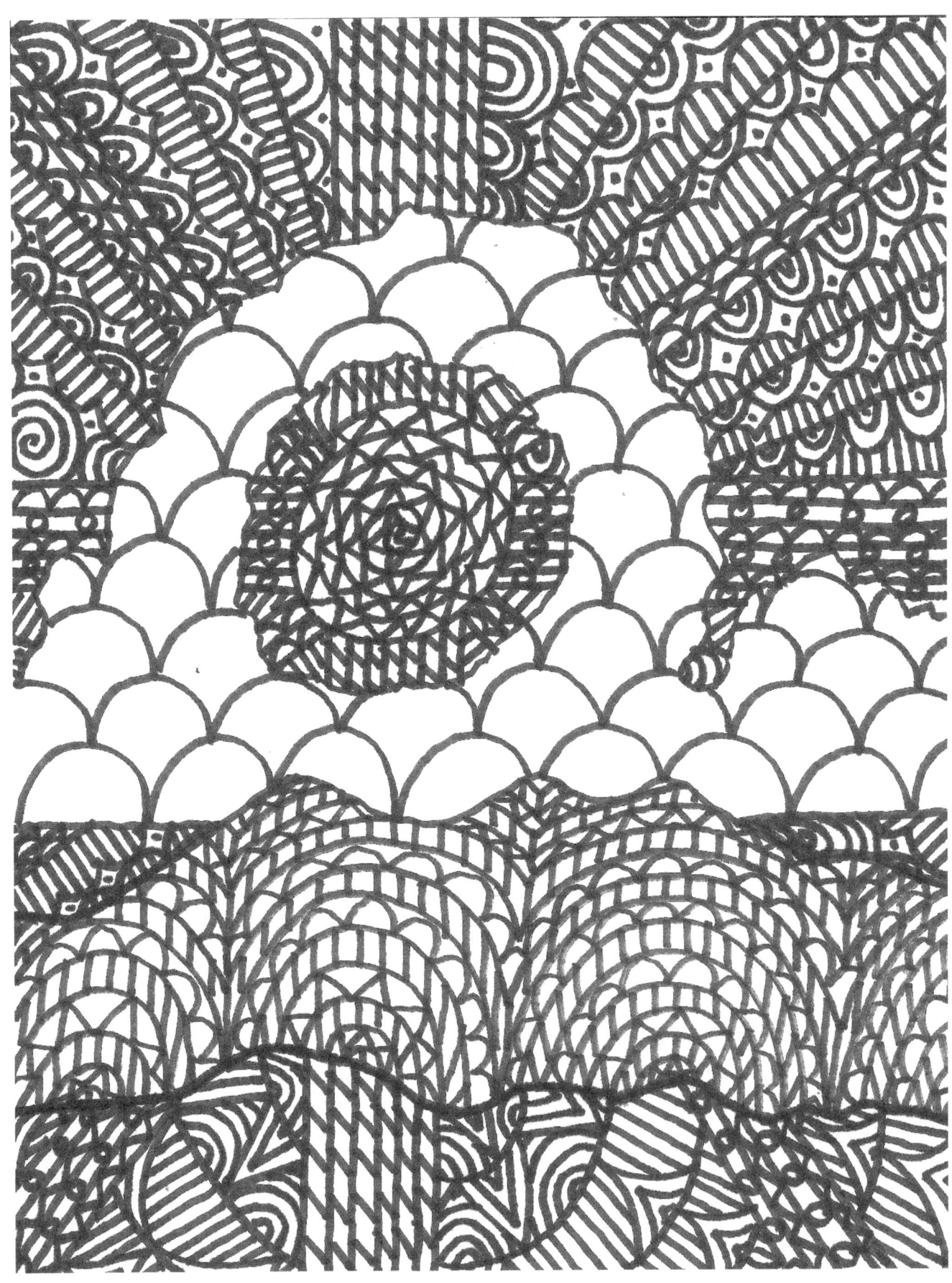

Bobby J. Jones

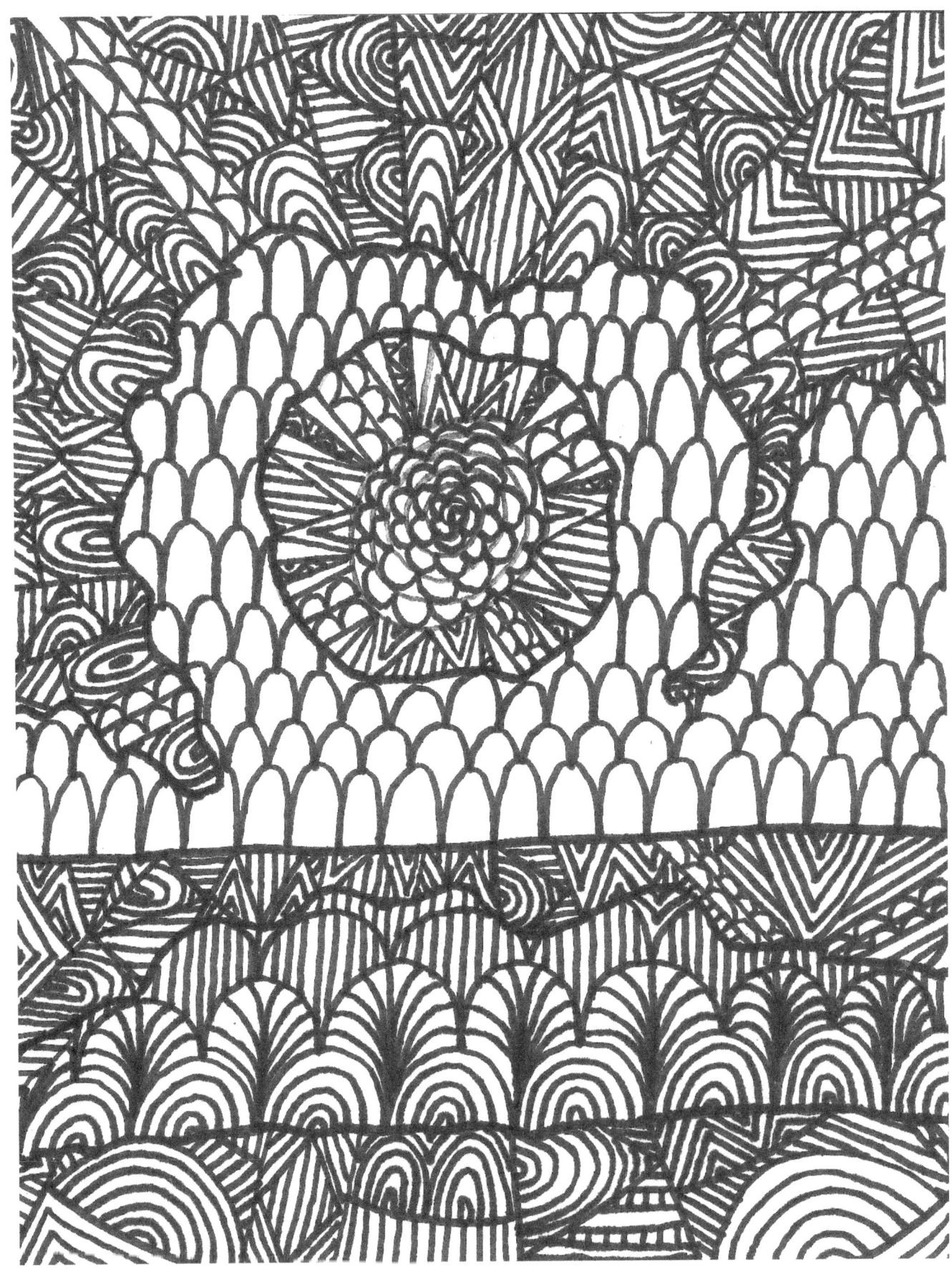

Bobby J. Jones

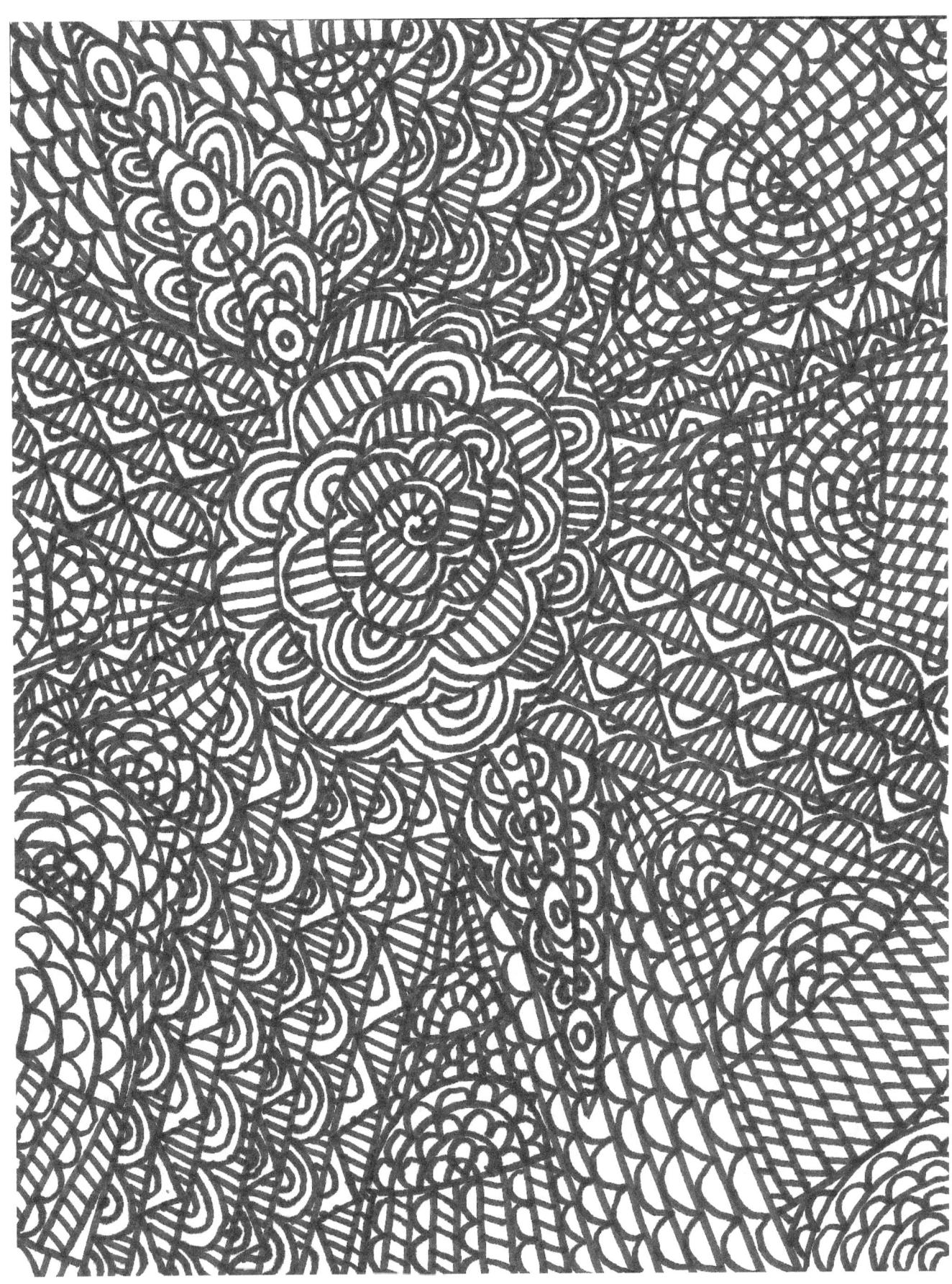

New Mexico Dreamscapes

Bobby J. Jones

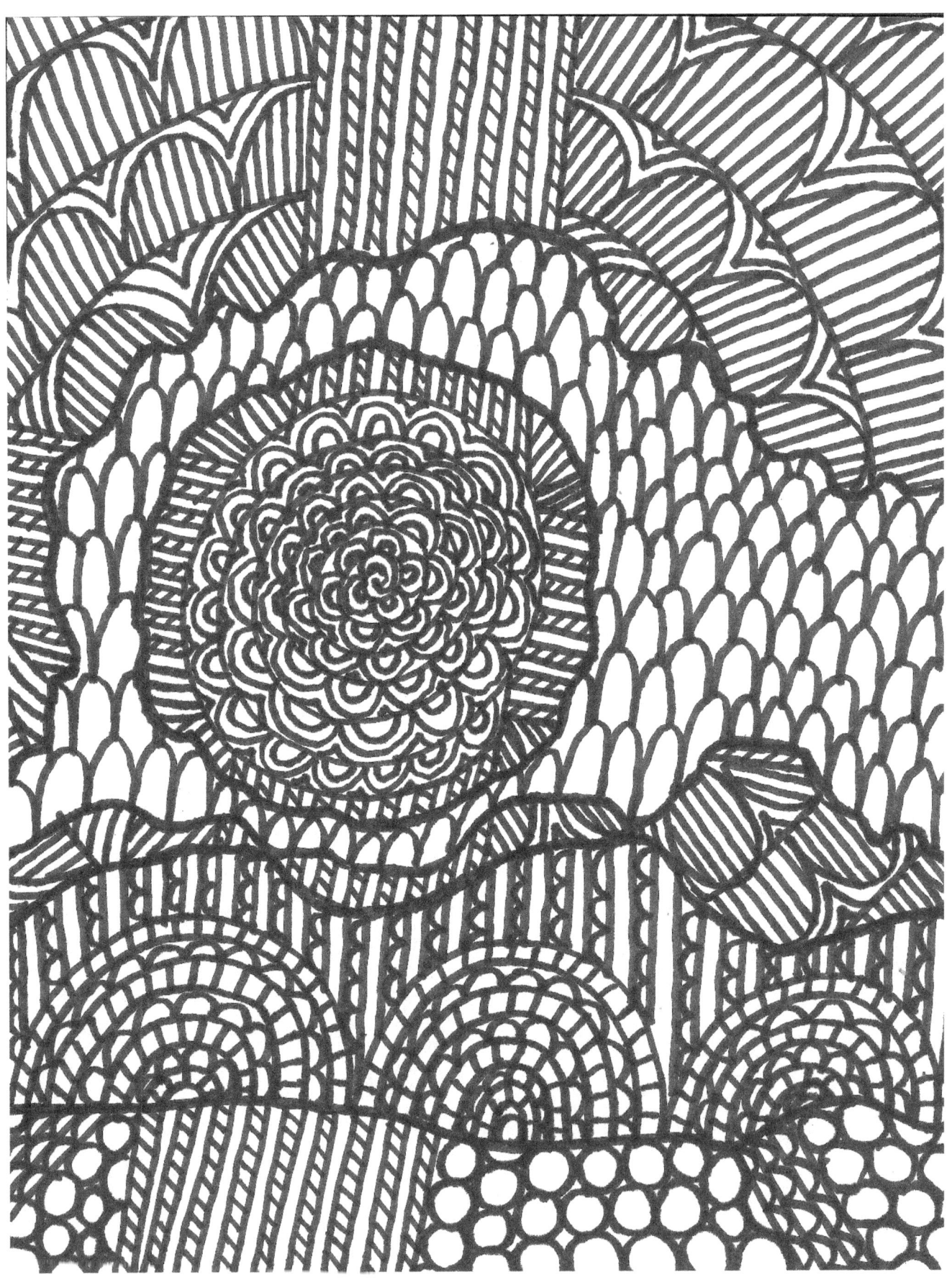

New Mexico Dreamscapes

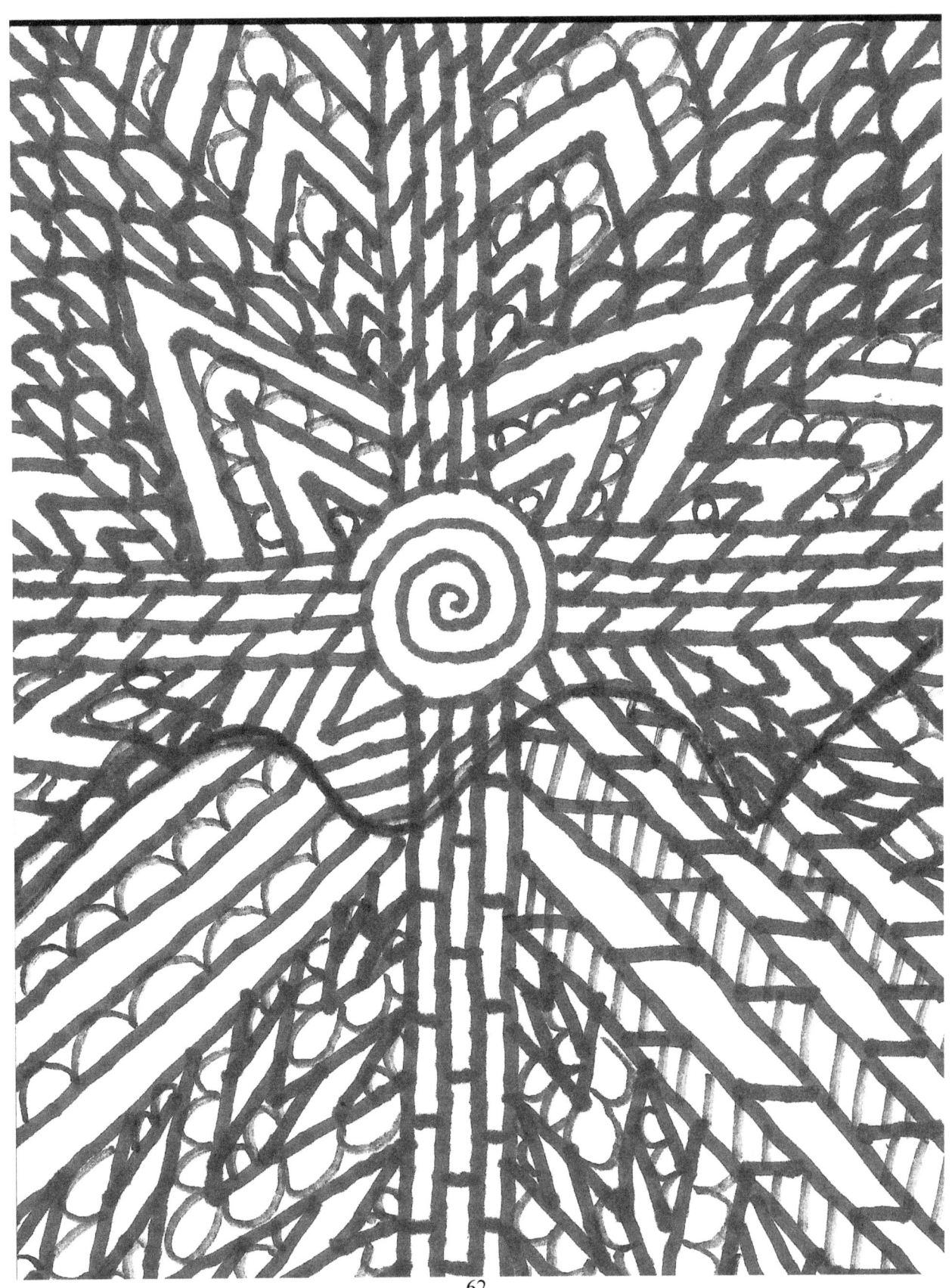

New Mexico Dreamscapes

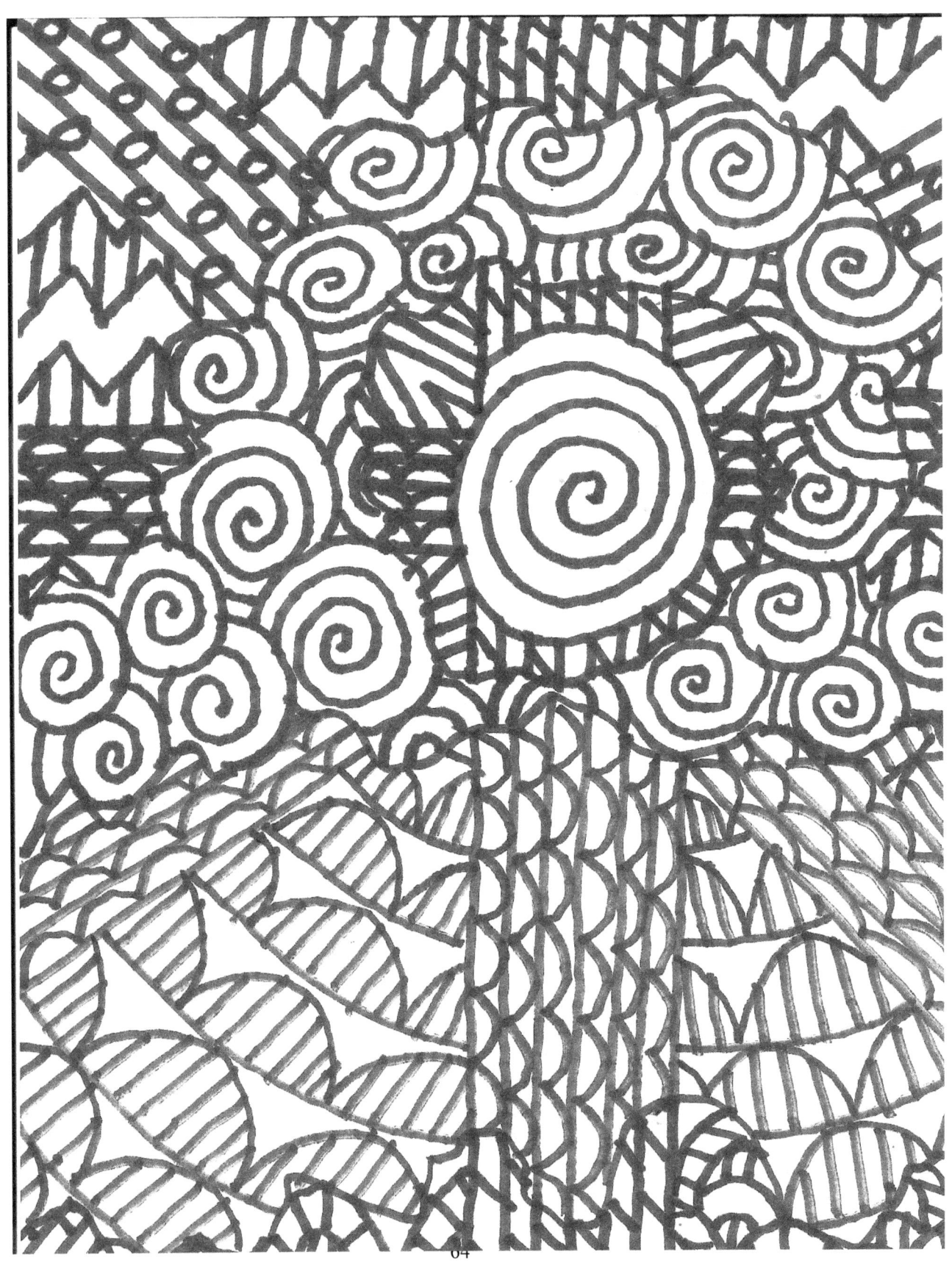

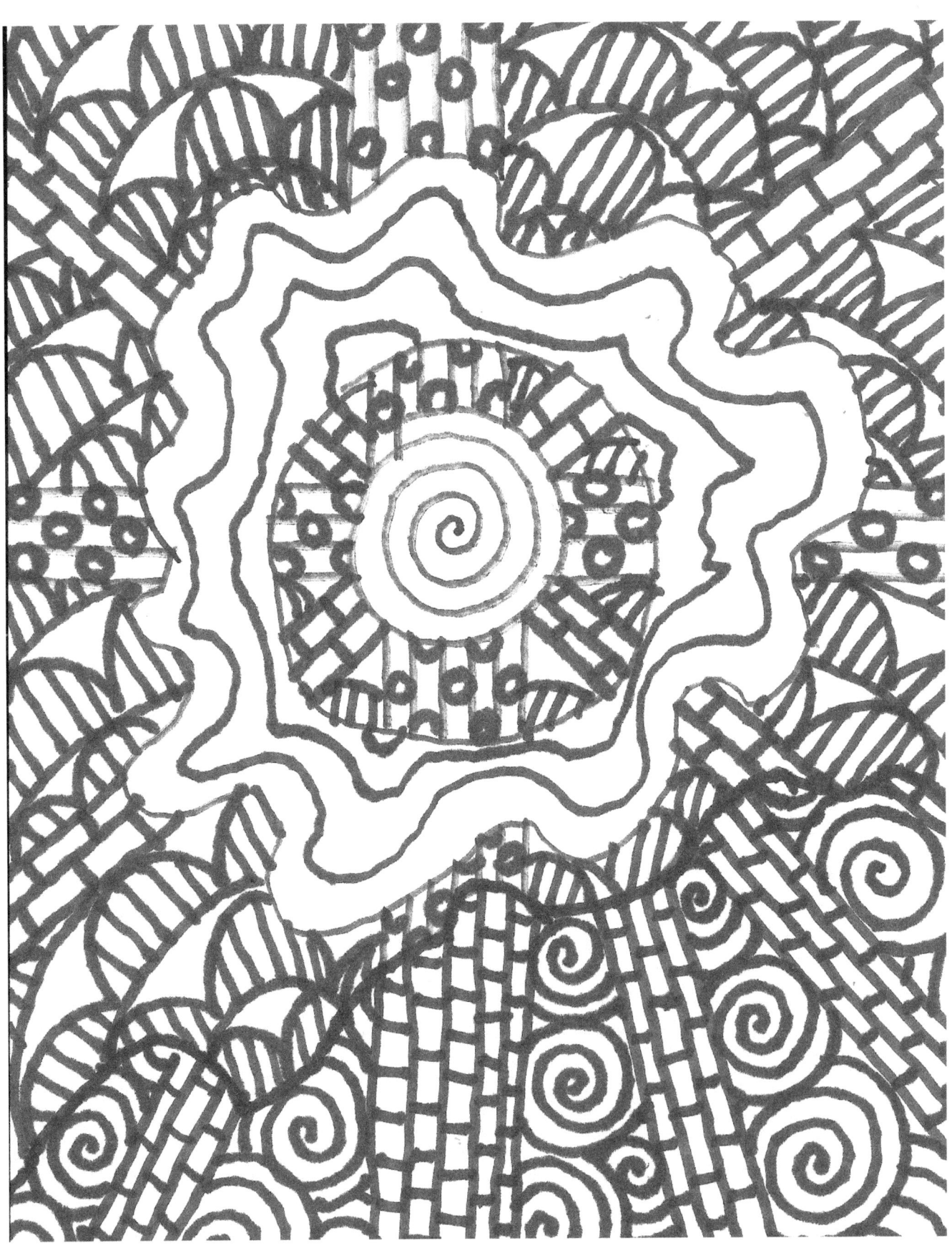

New Mexico Dreamscapes

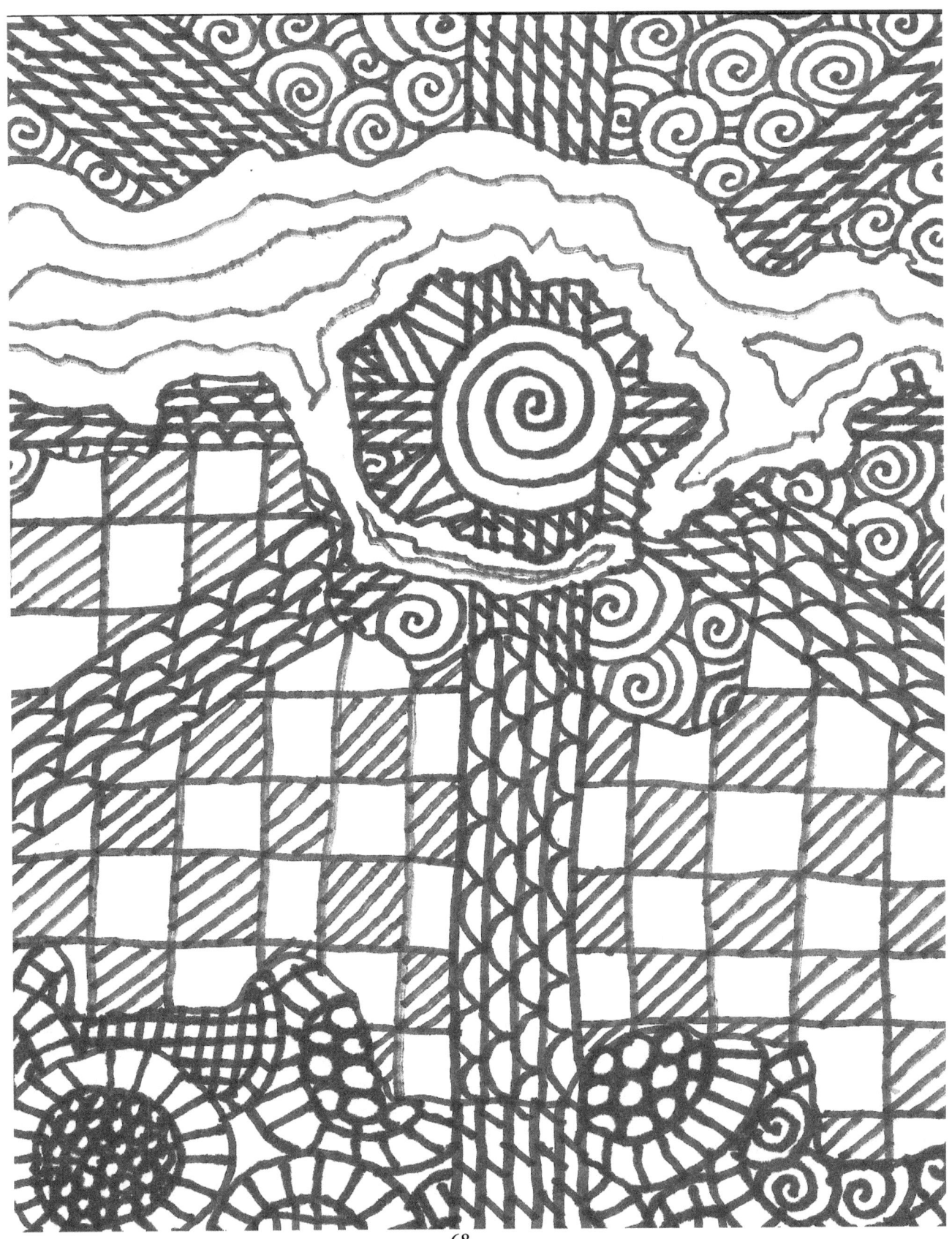

New Mexico Dreamscapes

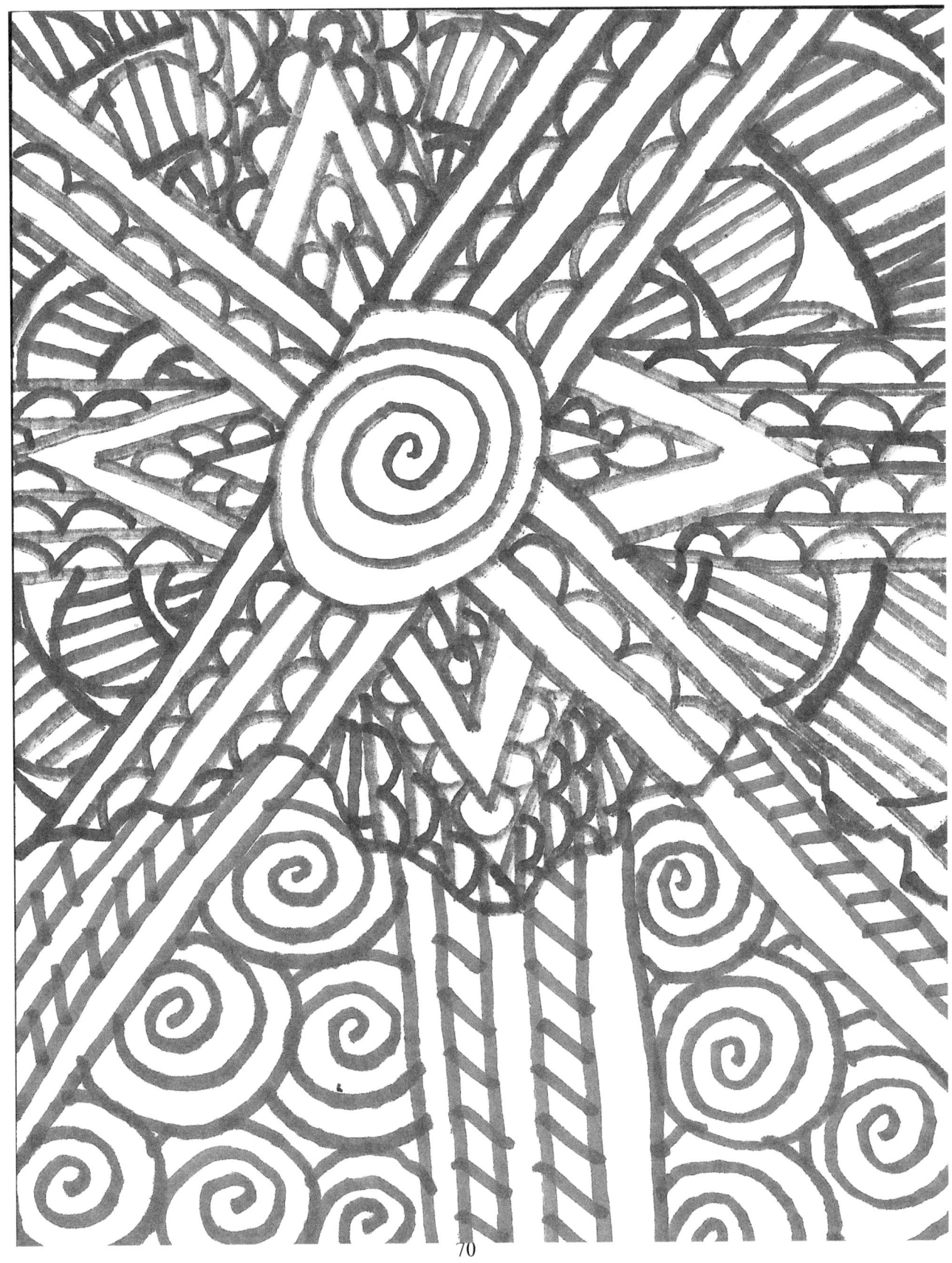

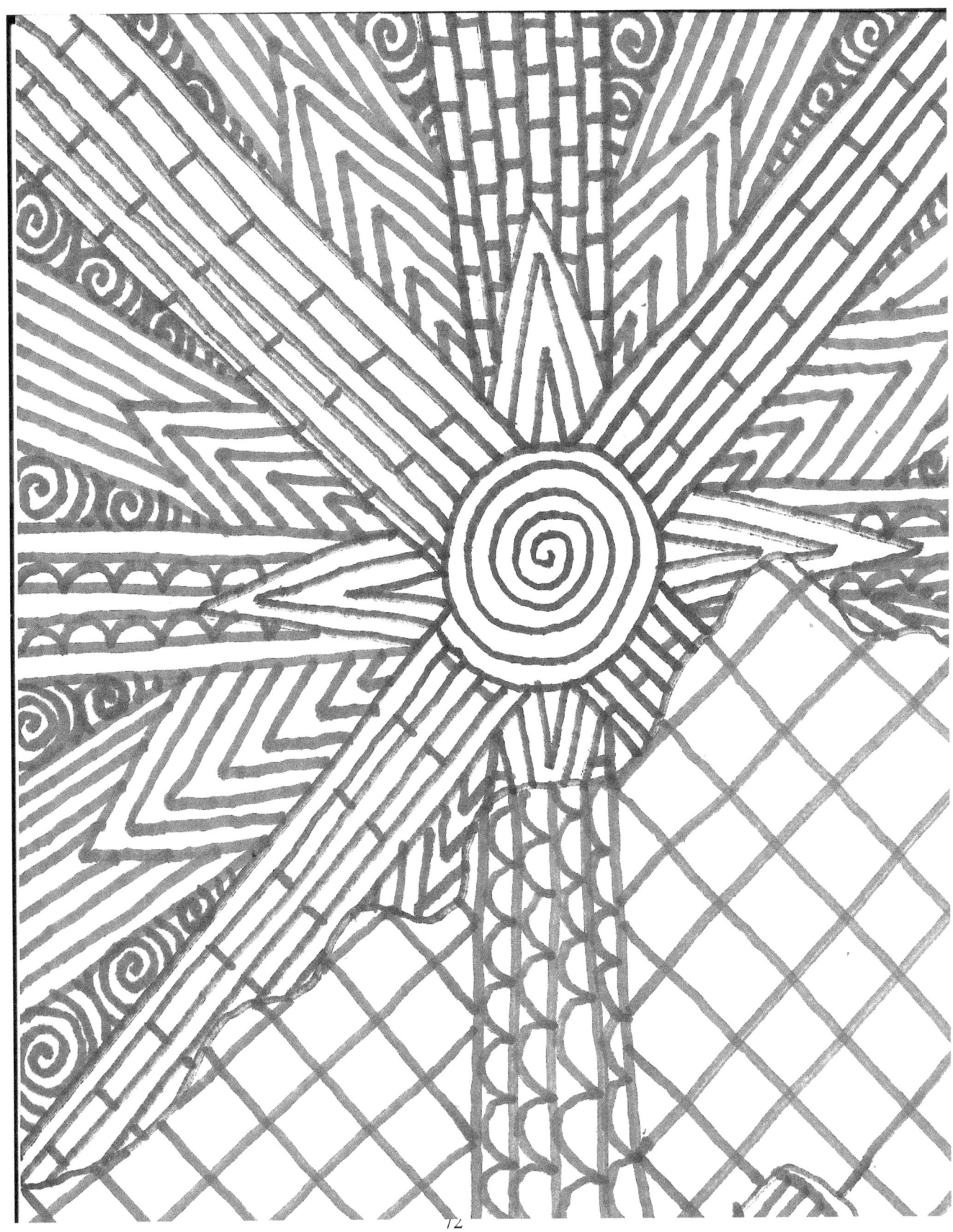

New Mexico Dreamscapes

Bobby J. Jones

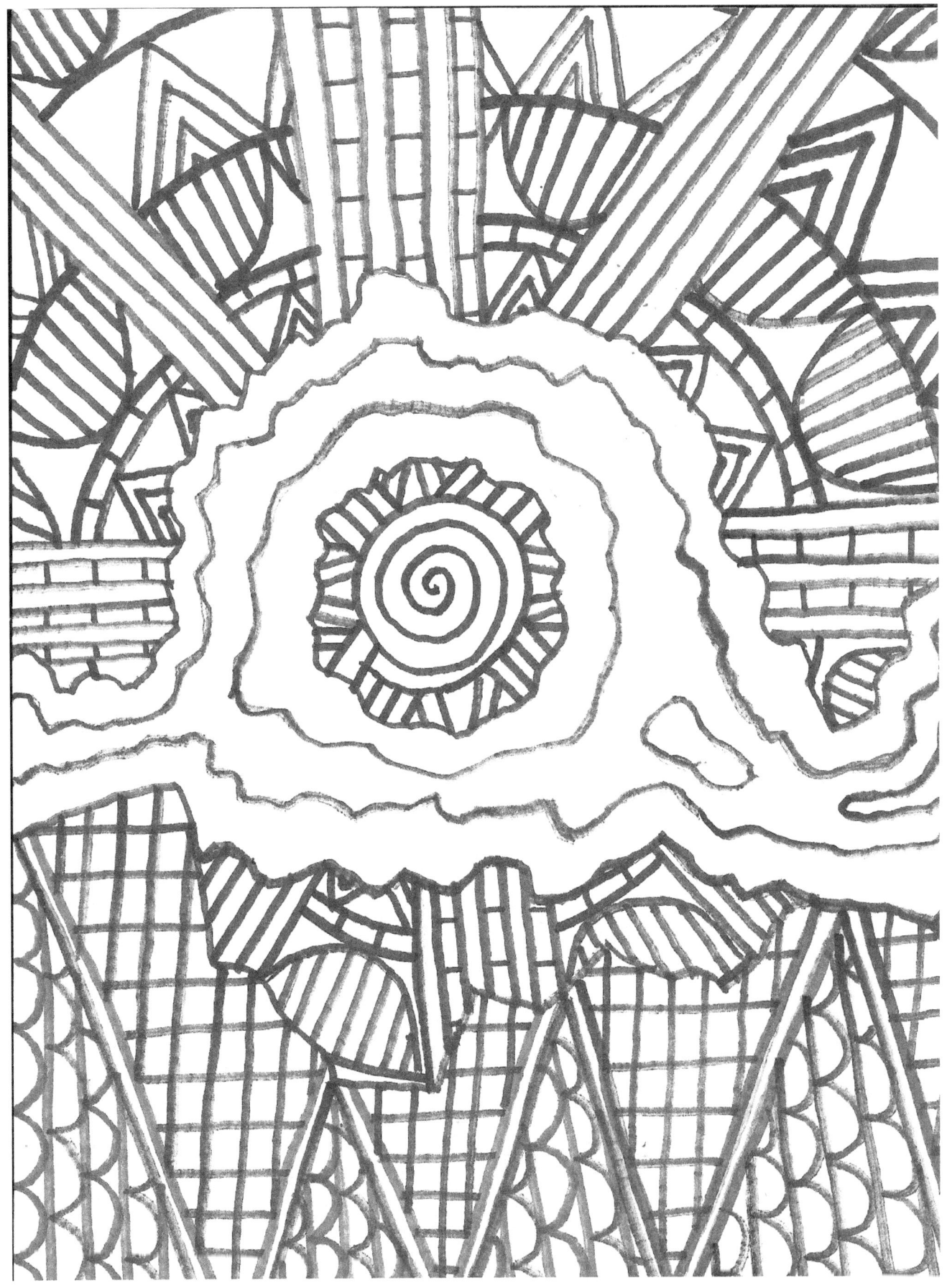

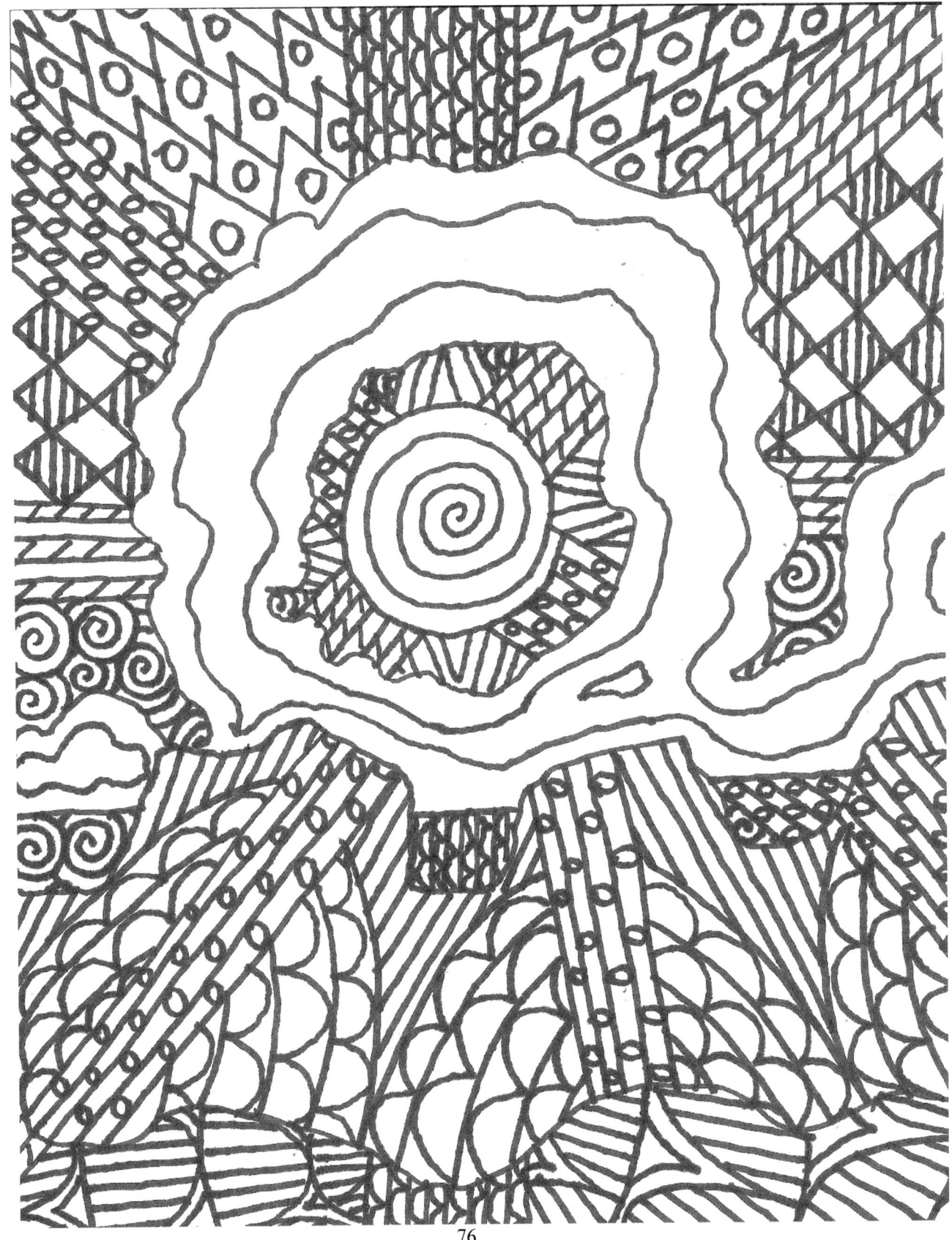

Bobby J. Jones

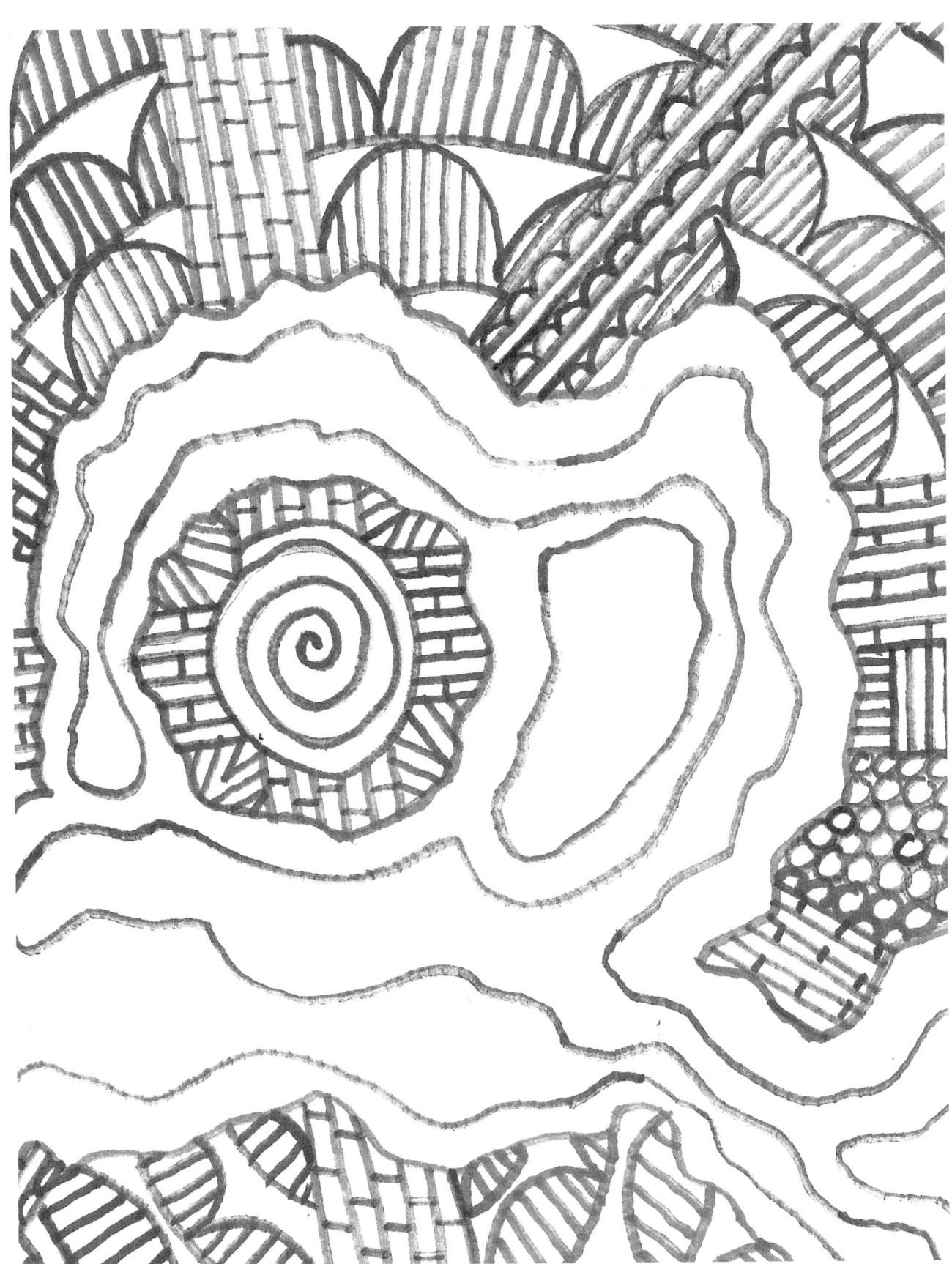

New Mexico Dreamscapes

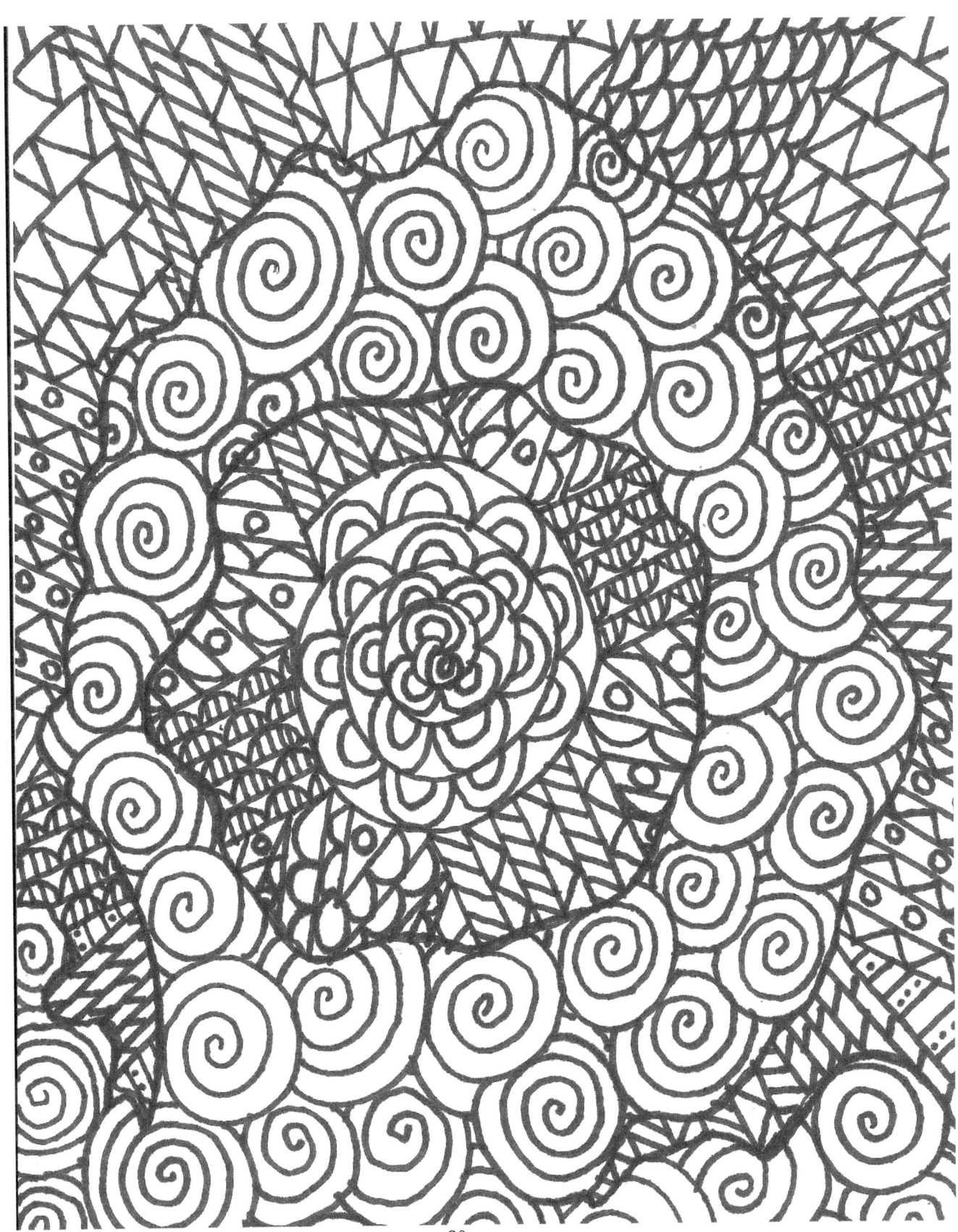

New Mexico Dreamscapes

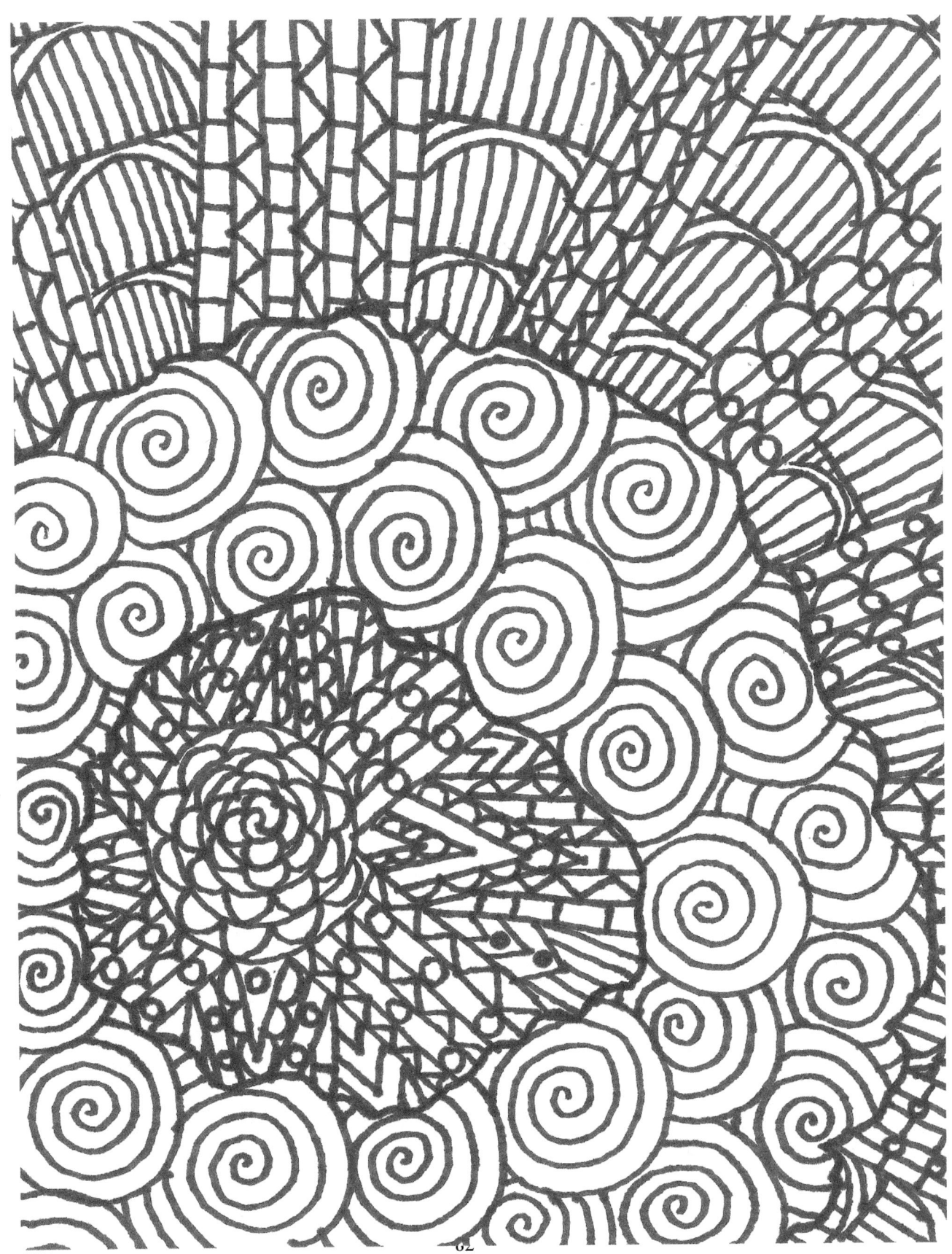

New Mexico Dreamscapes

Bobby J. Jones

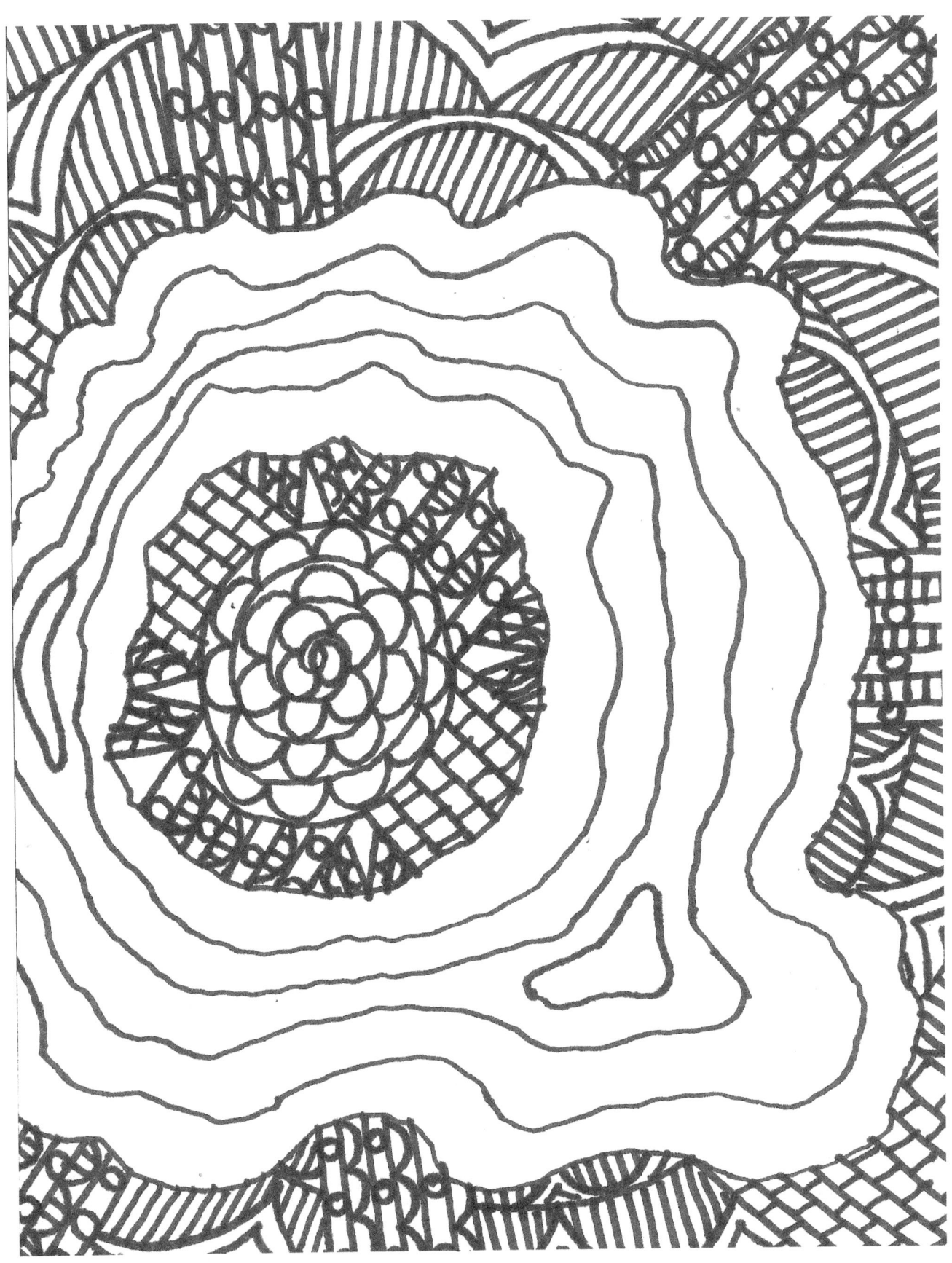

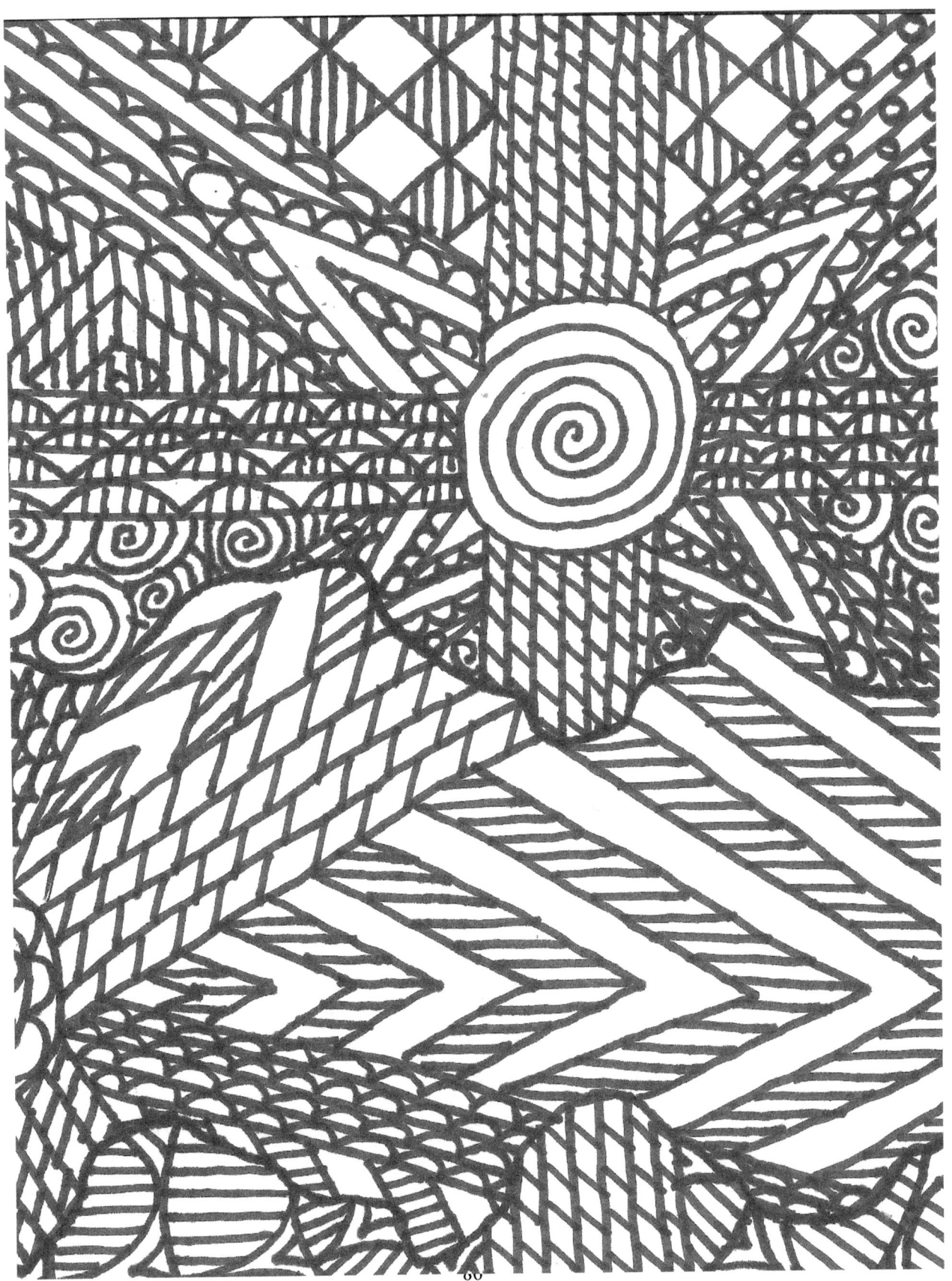

New Mexico Dreamscapes

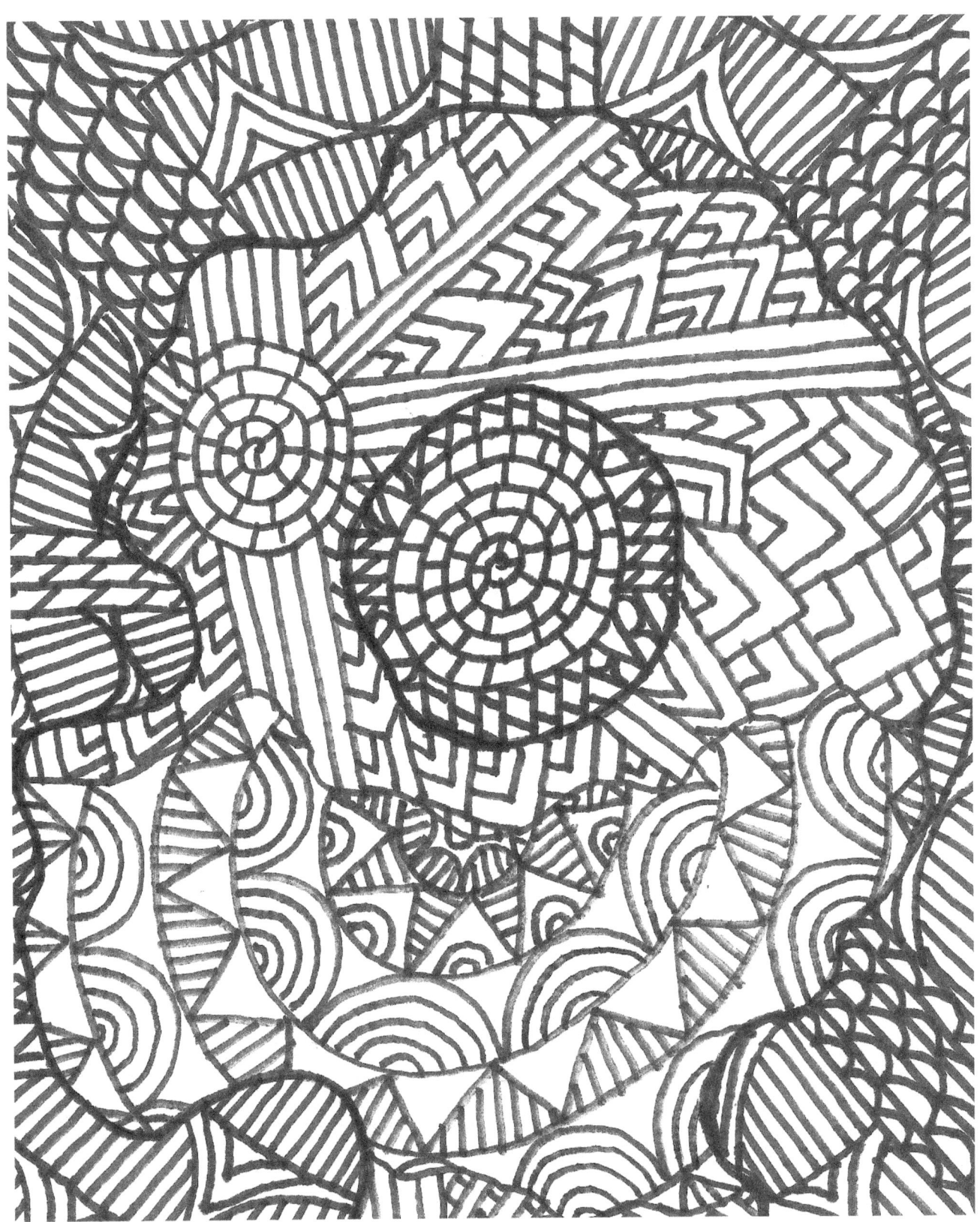

New Mexico Dreamscapes

Bobby J. Jones

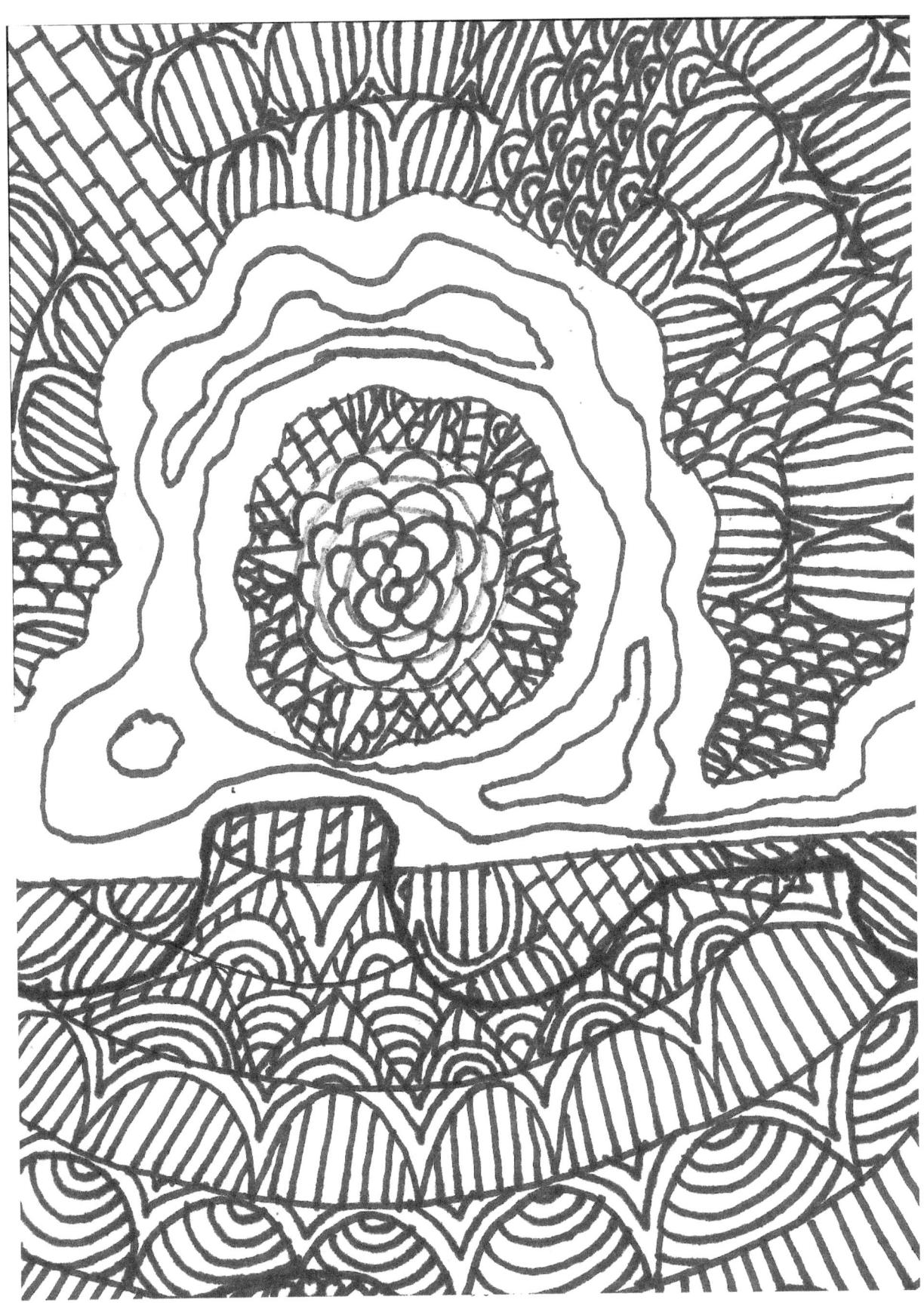

New Mexico Dreamscapes

Bobby J. Jones

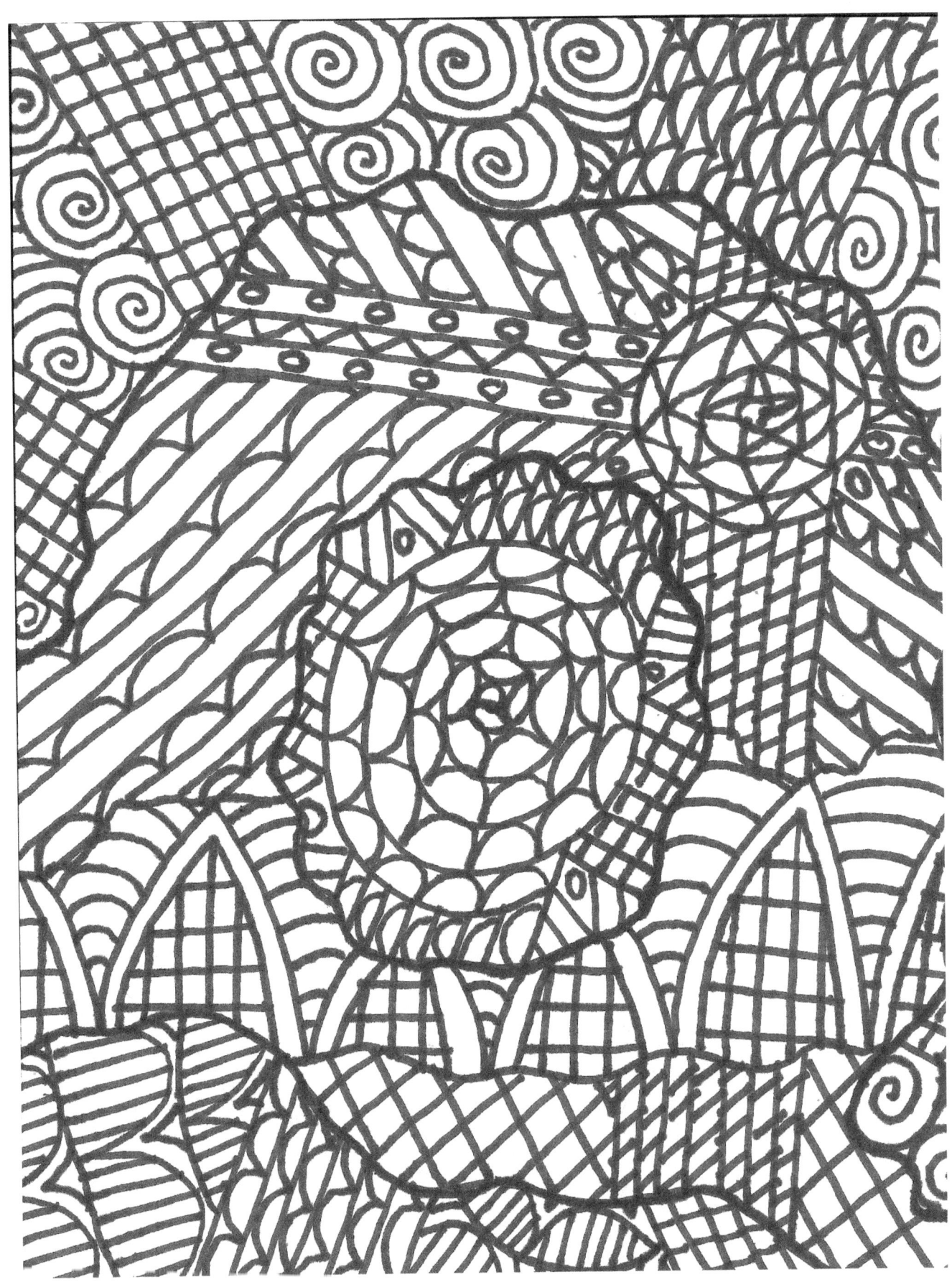

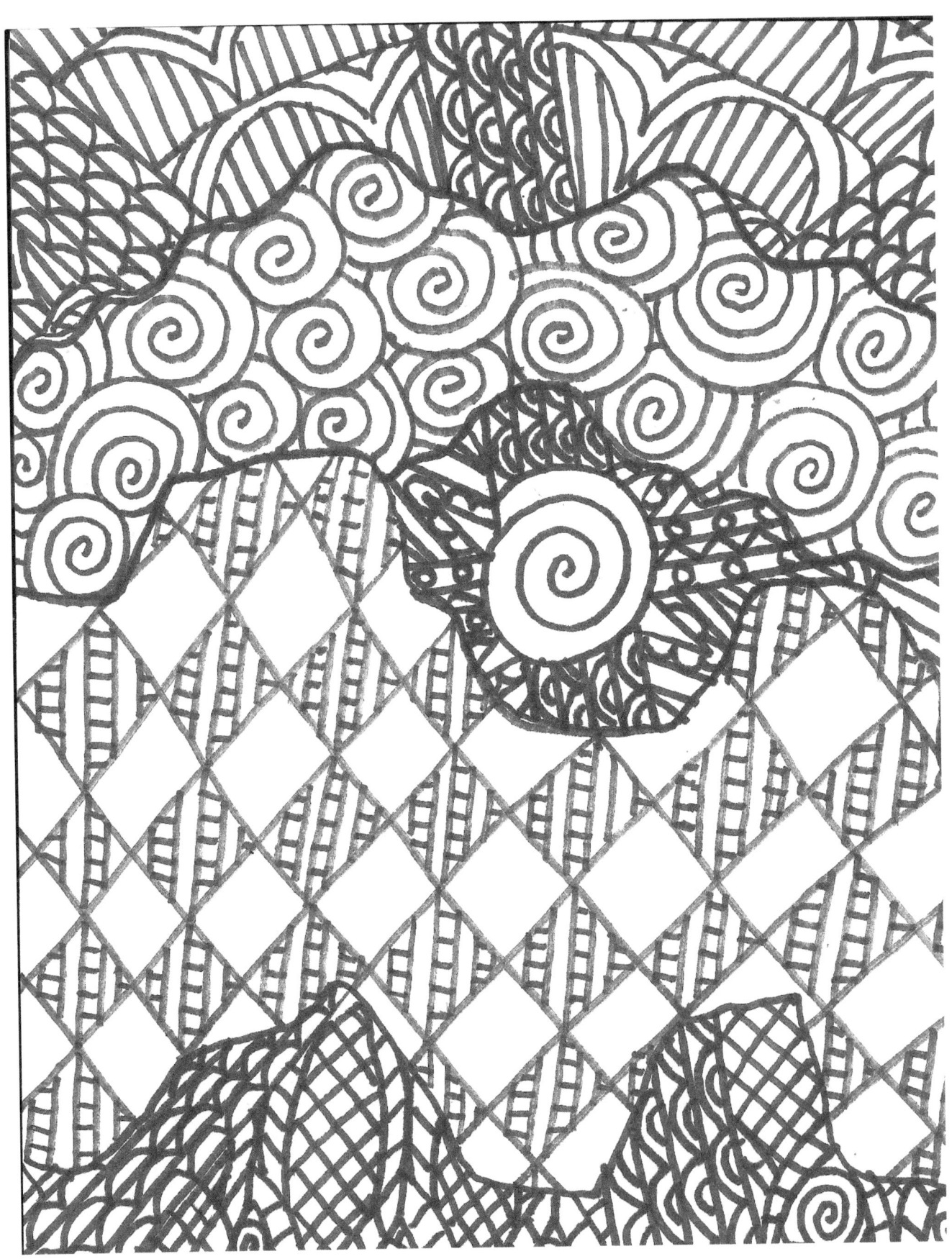

Bobby J. Jones

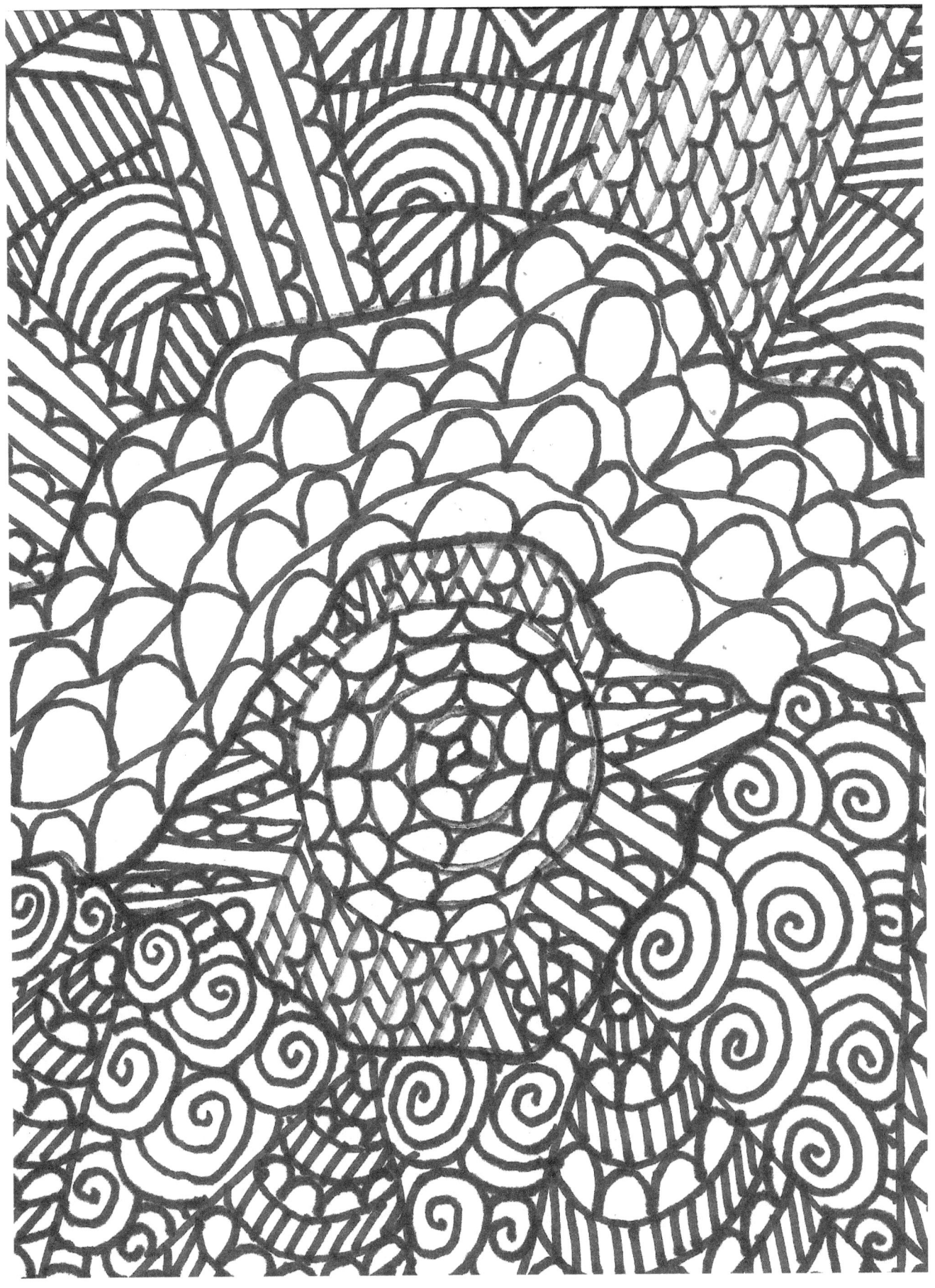

Bobby J. Jones

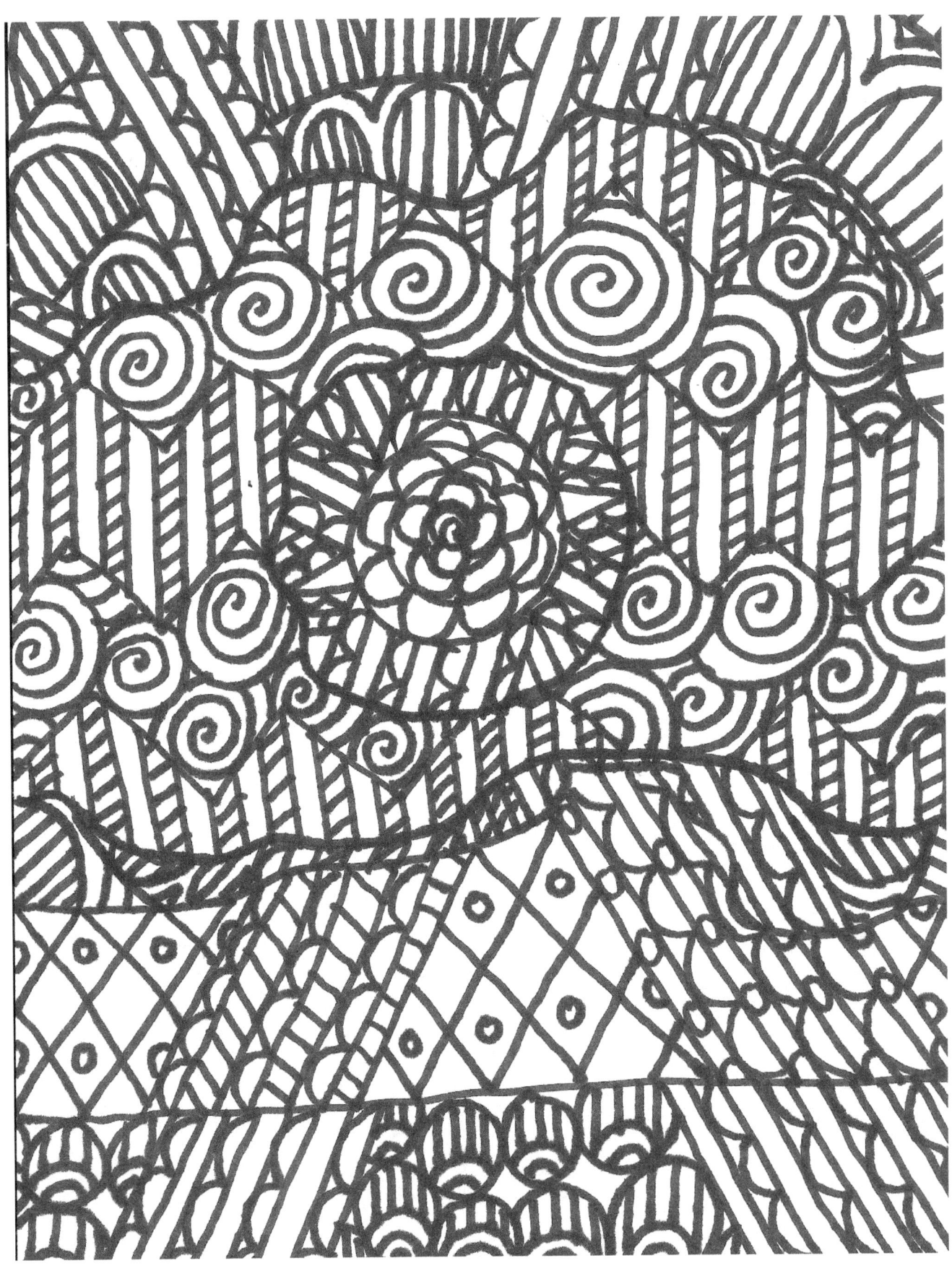

New Mexico Dreamscapes

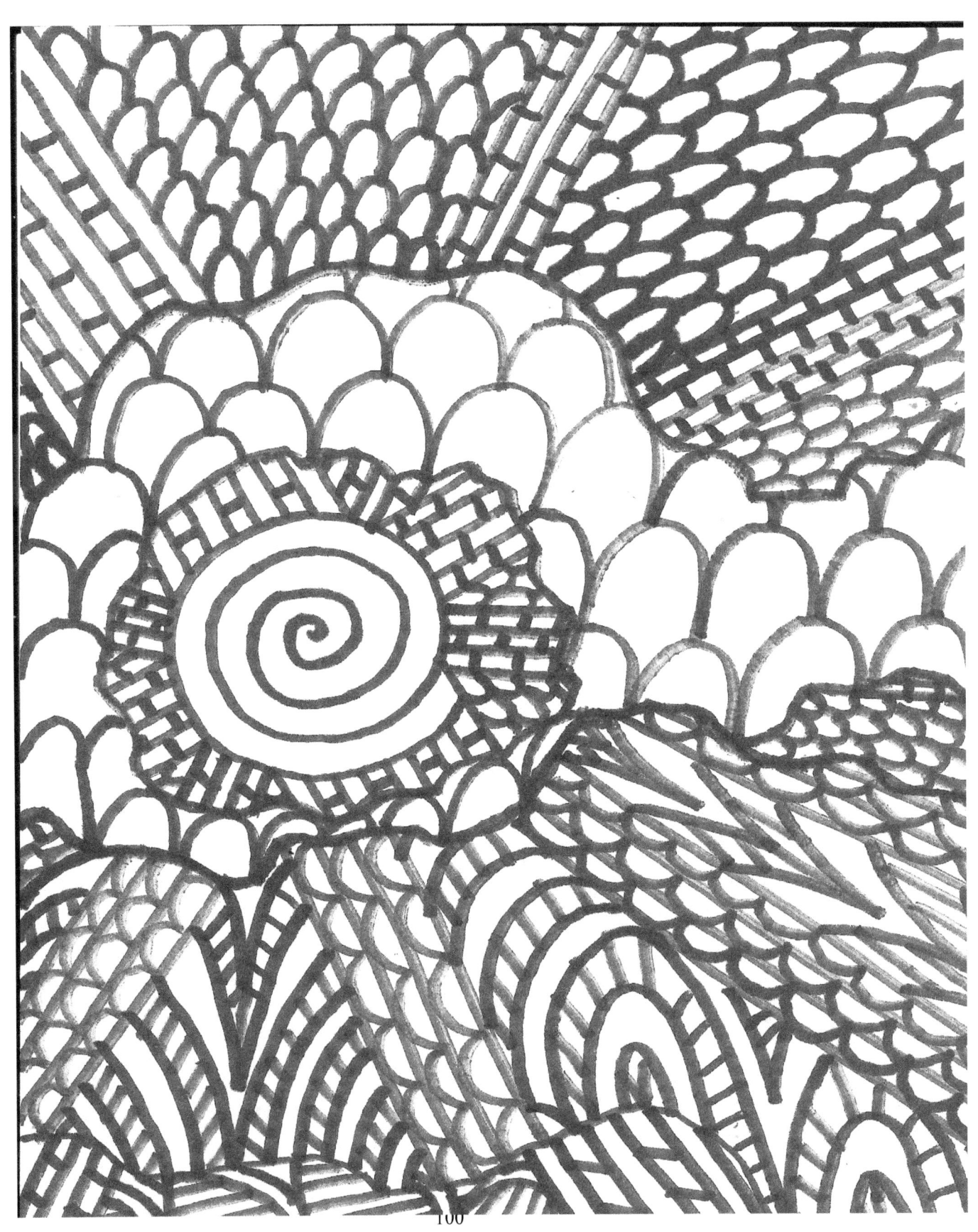

Bobby J. Jones

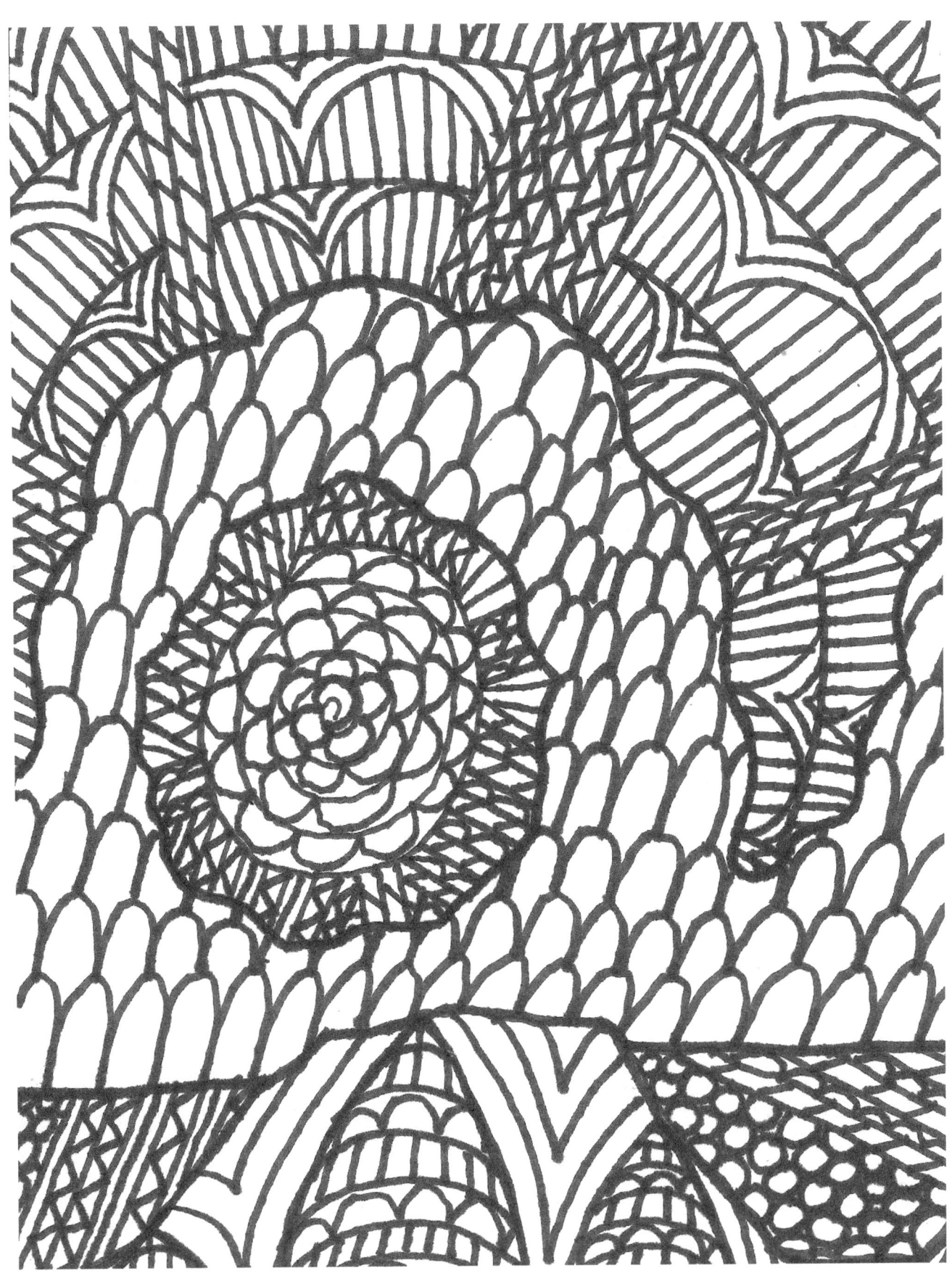

New Mexico Dreamscapes

Bobby J. Jones

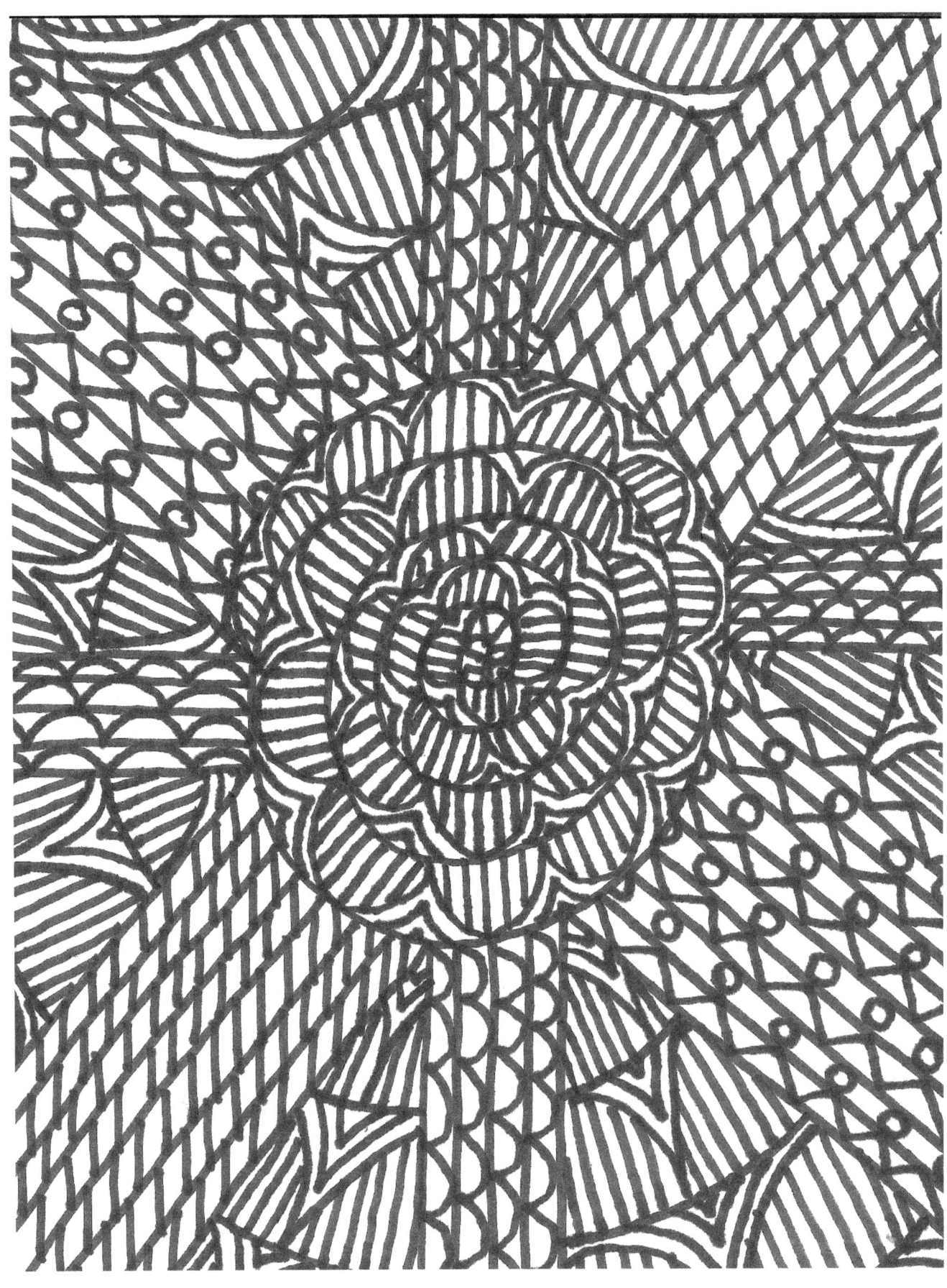

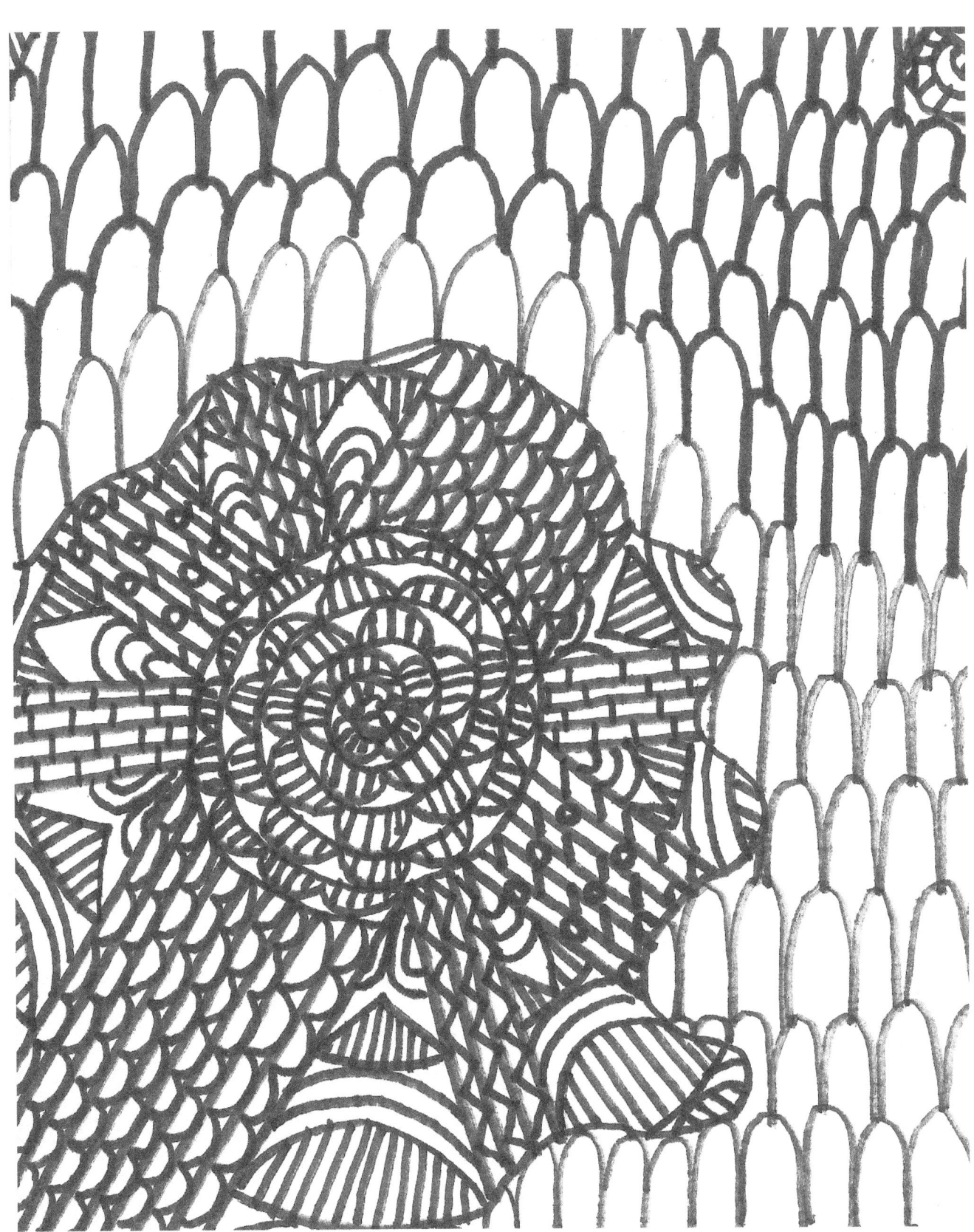

Bobby J. Jones

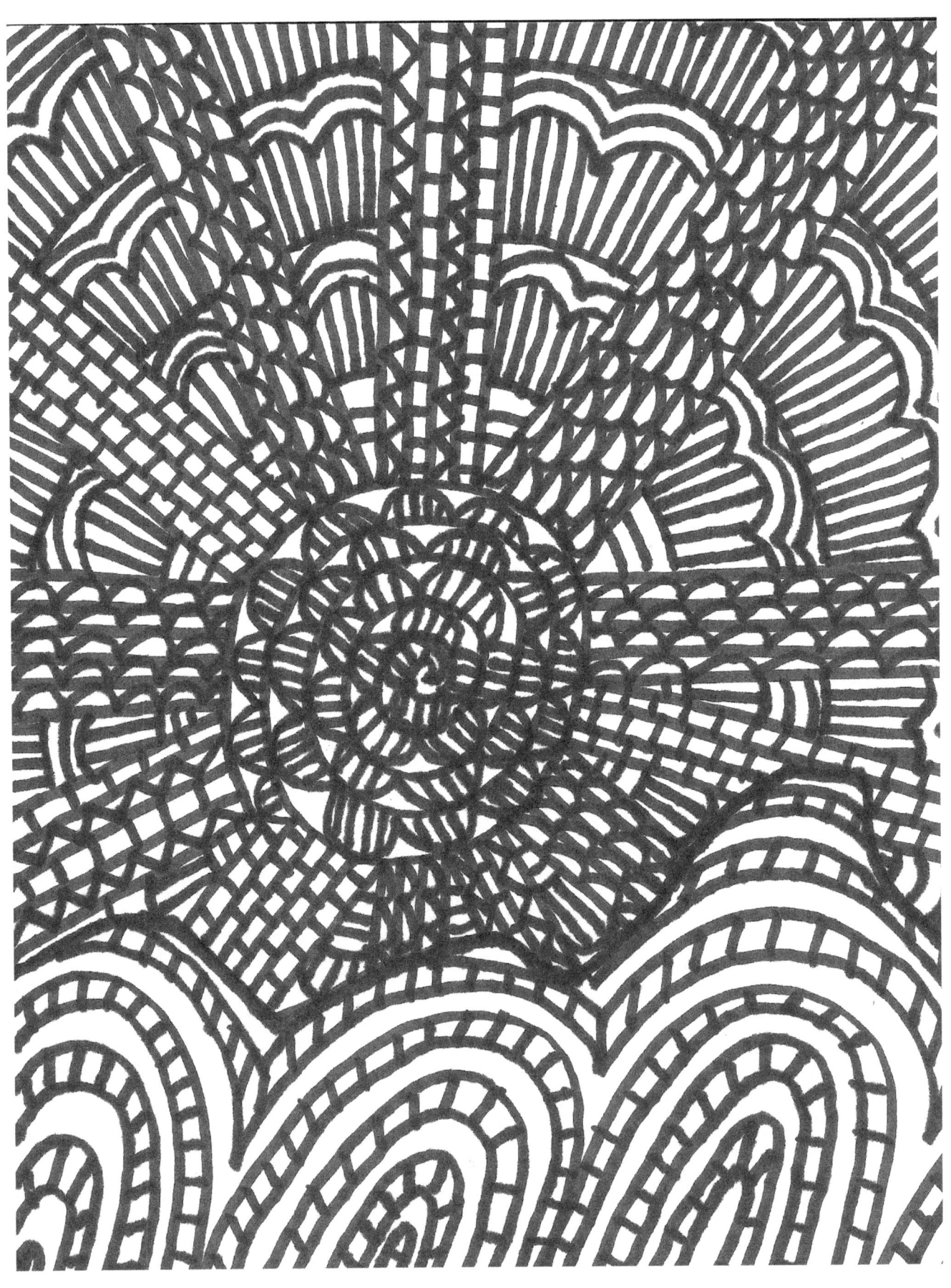

Bobby J. Jones

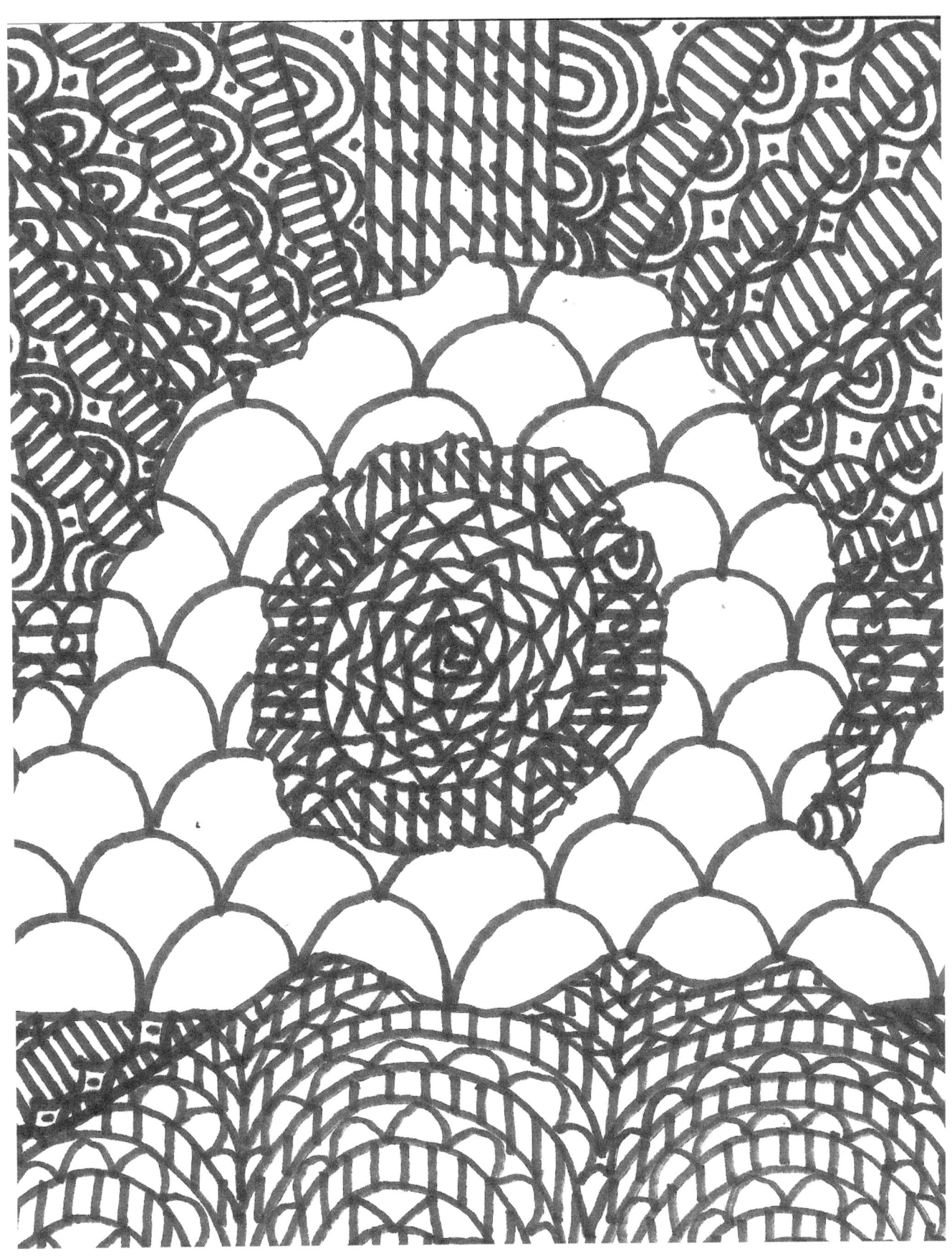

New Mexico Dreamscapes

Bobby J. Jones

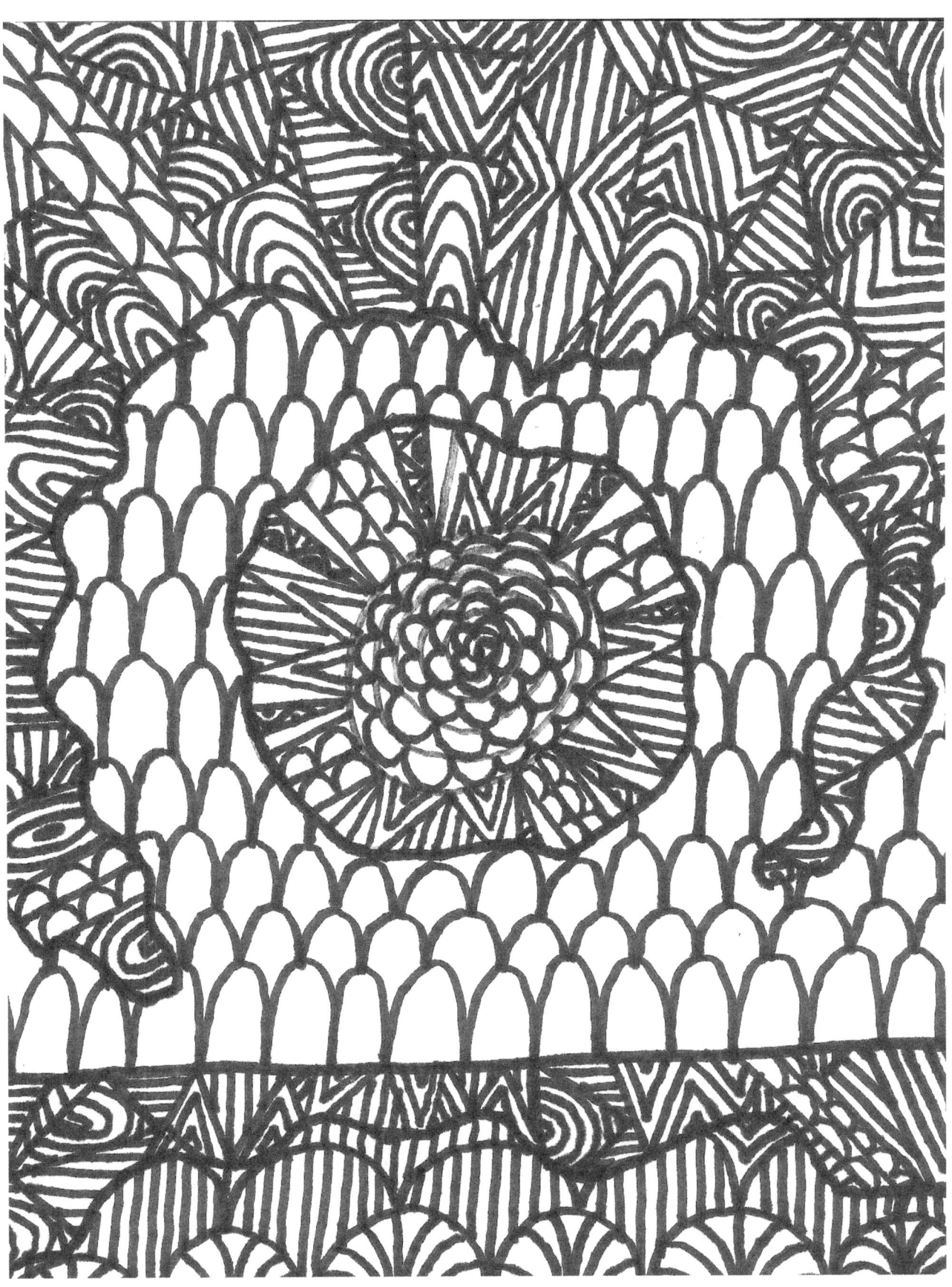

Bobby J. Jones

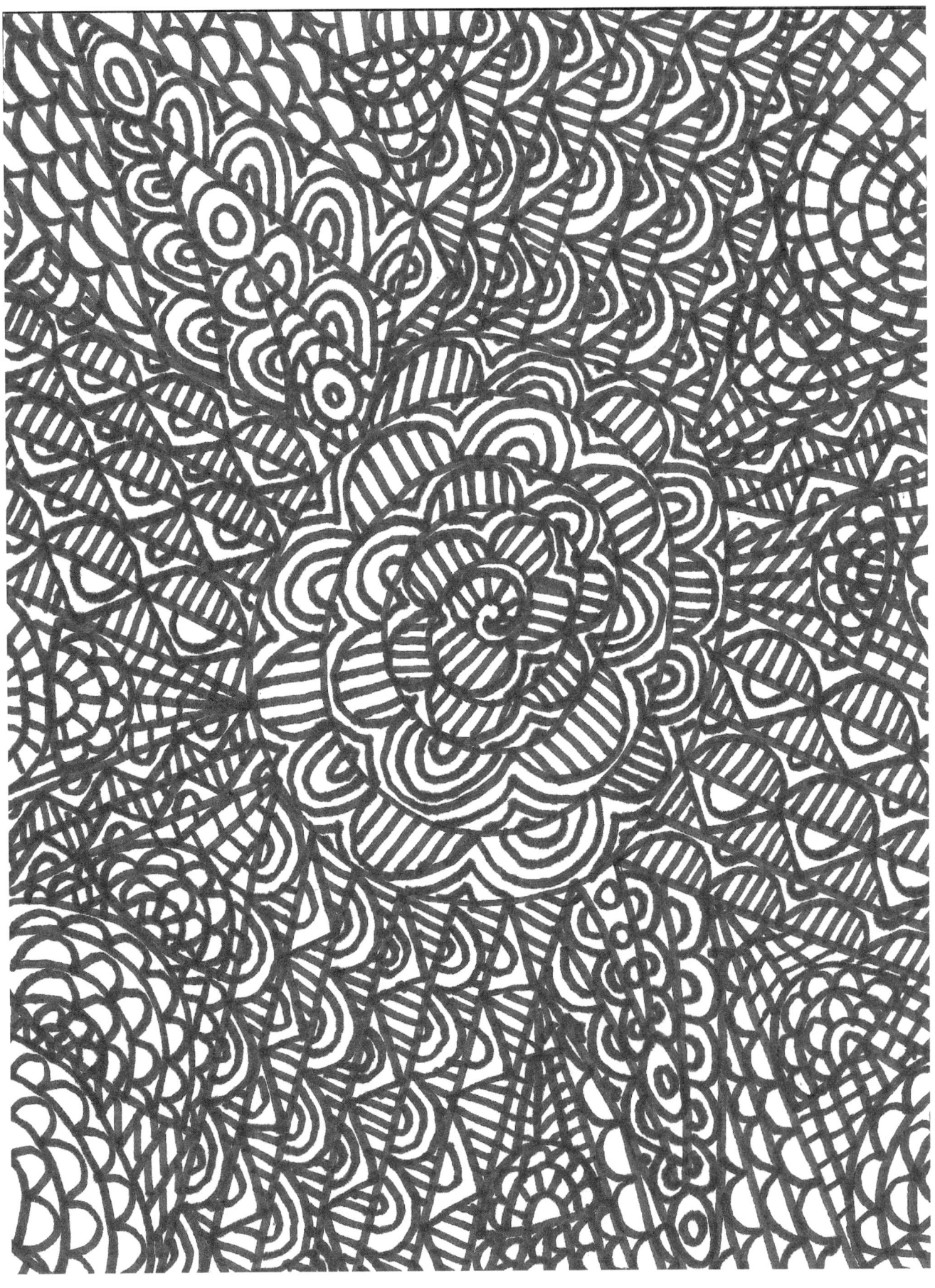

New Mexico Dreamscapes

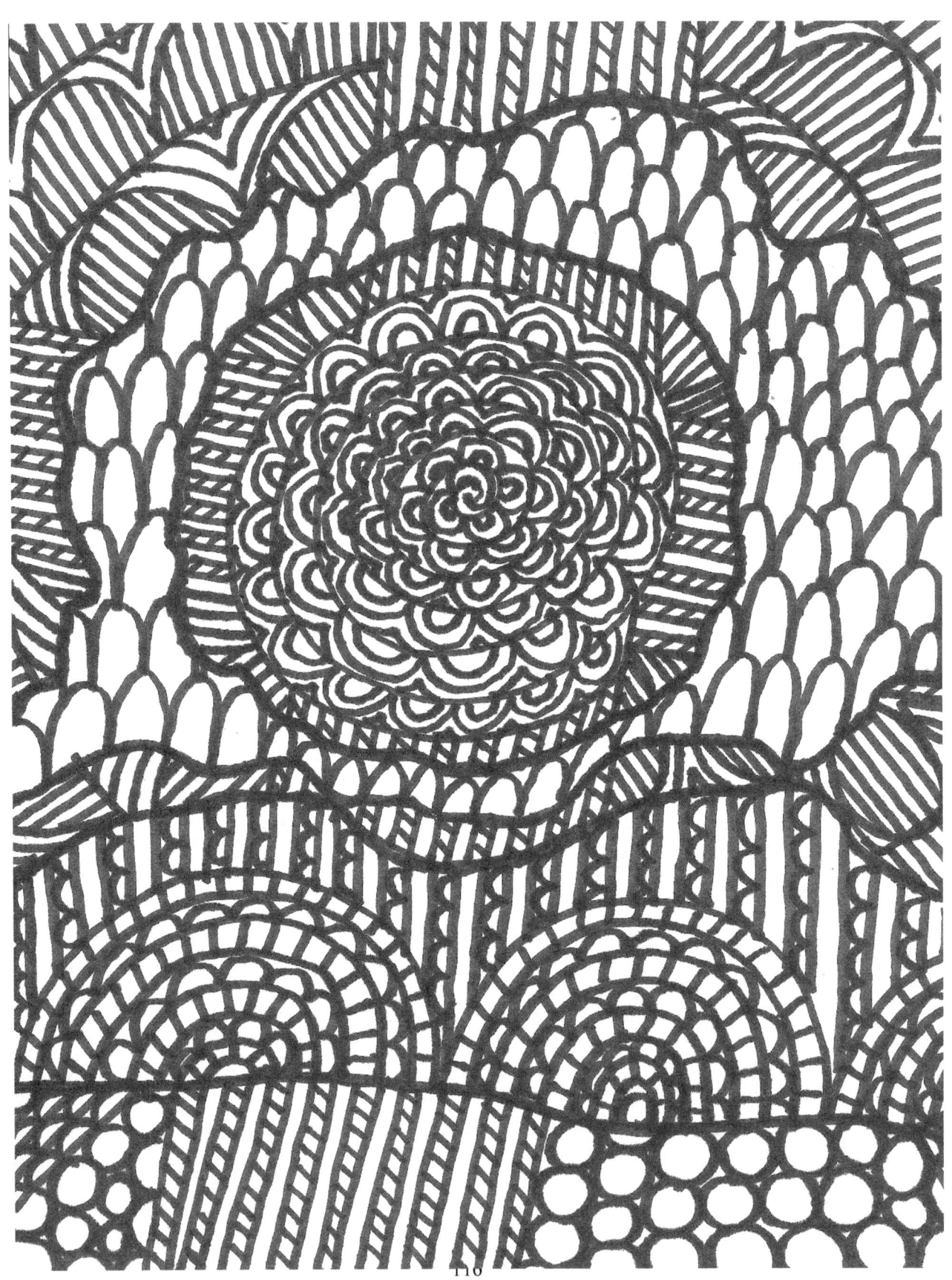

Bobby J. Jones

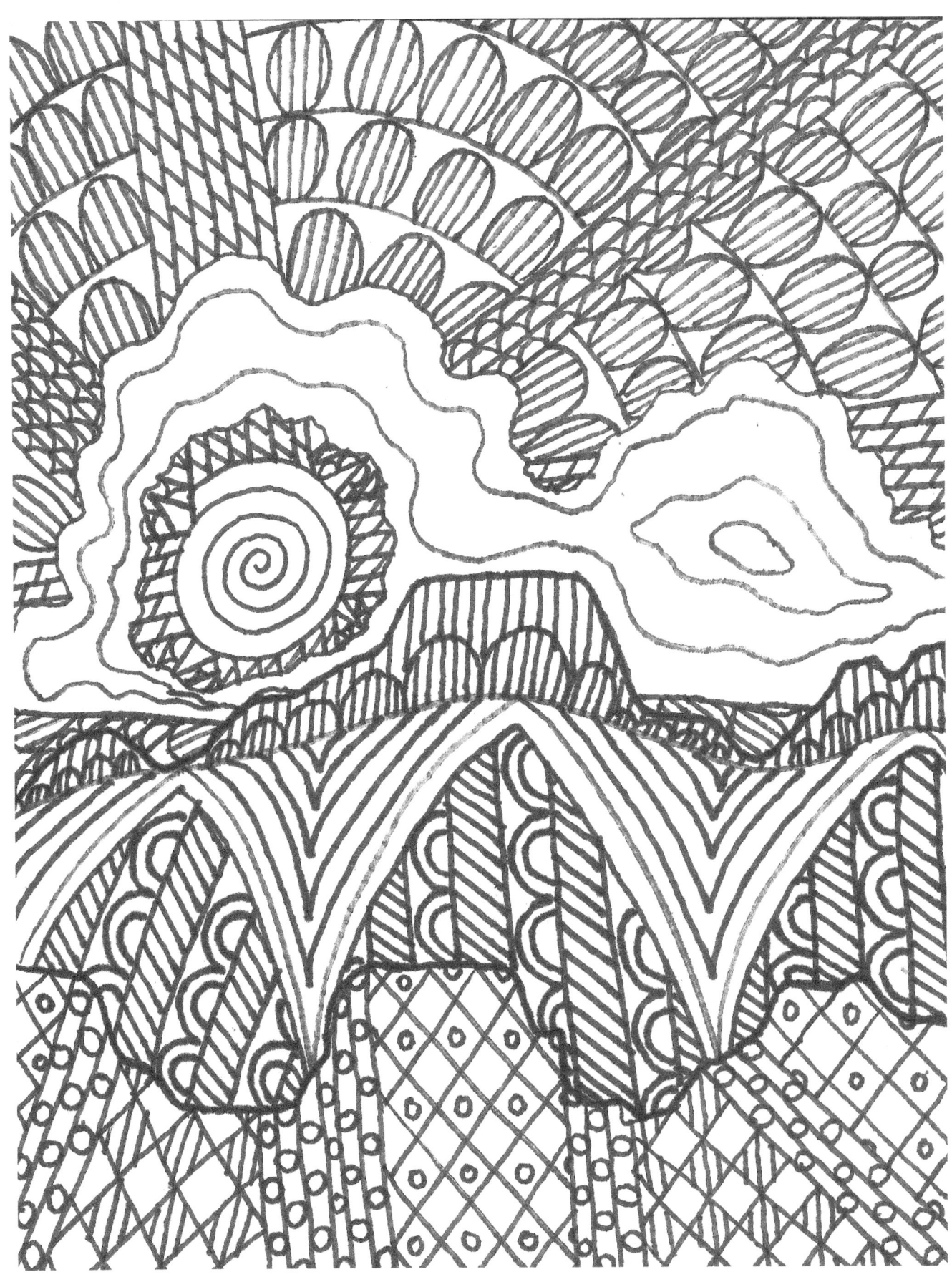

New Mexico Dreamscapes

Bobby J. Jones

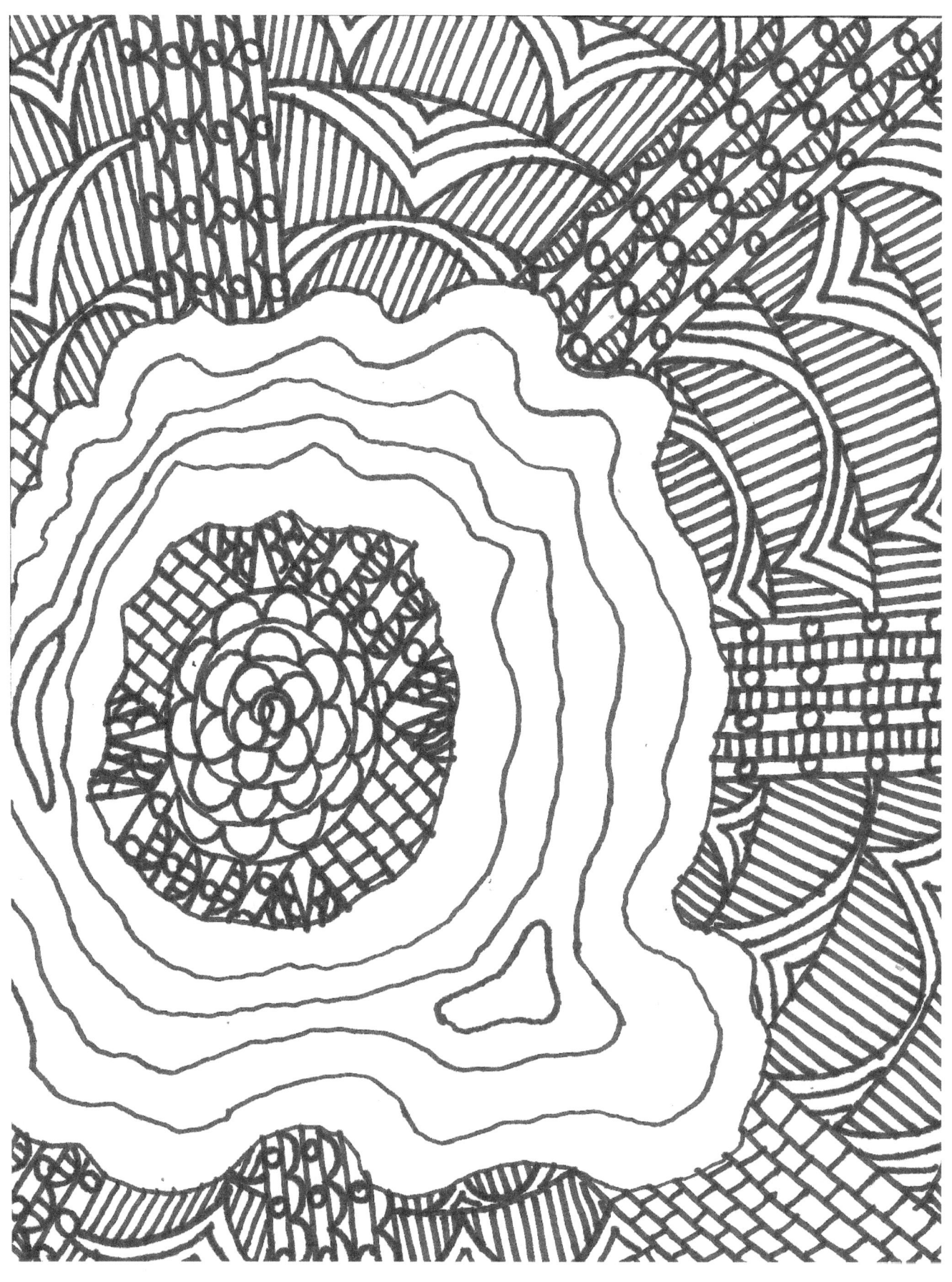

New Mexico Dreamscapes

Bobby J. Jones

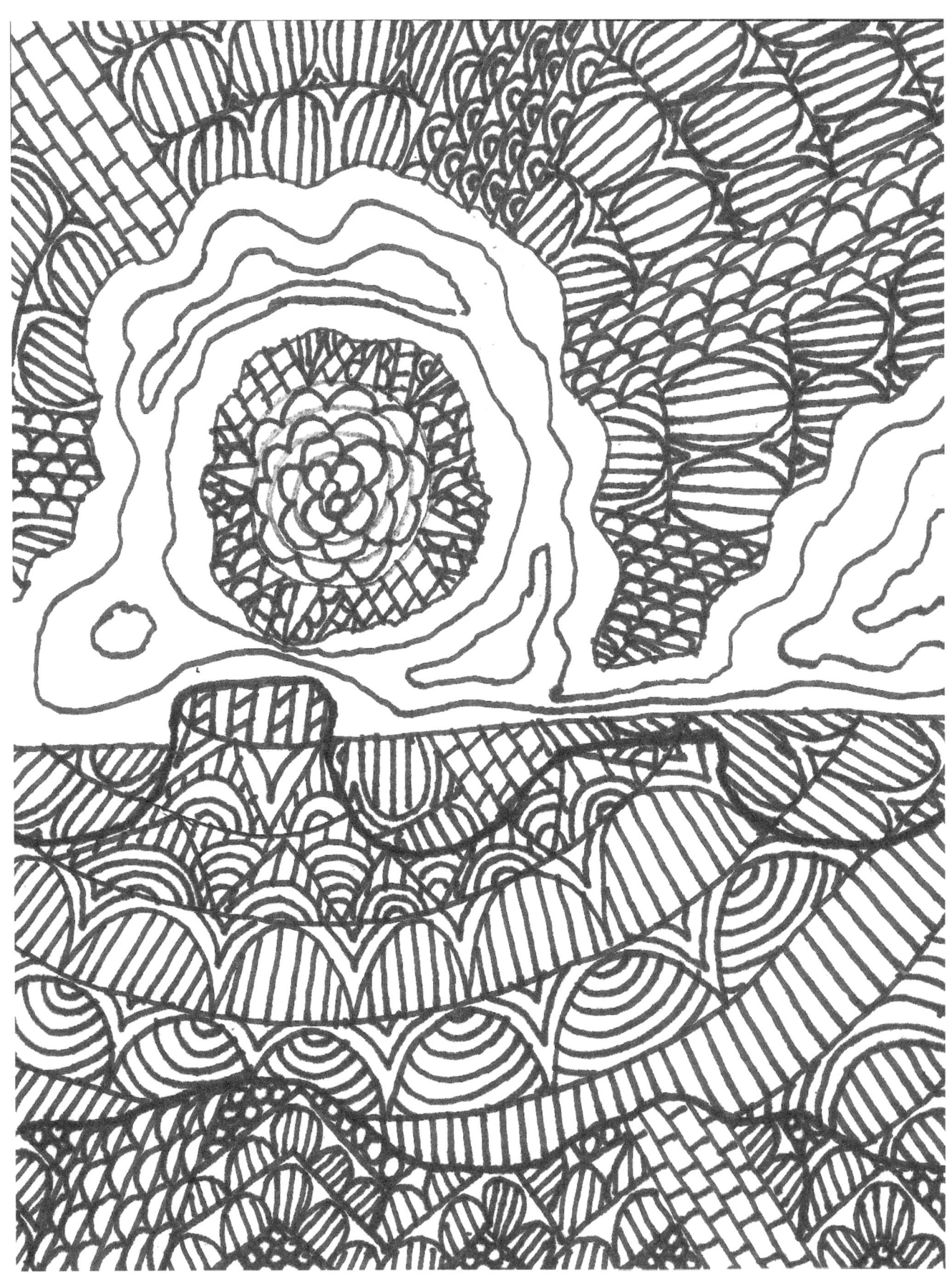

Bobby J. Jones

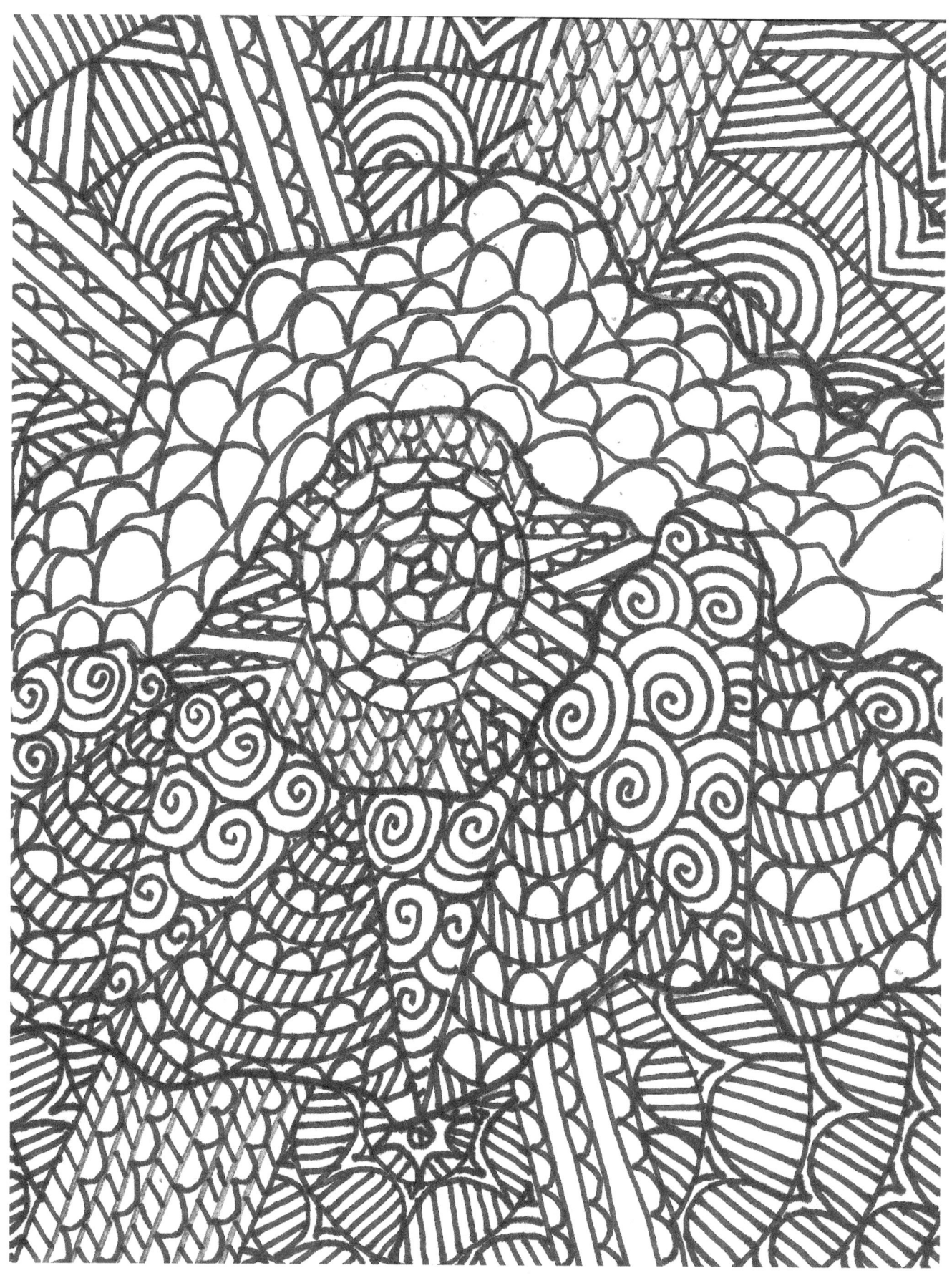

New Mexico Dreamscapes

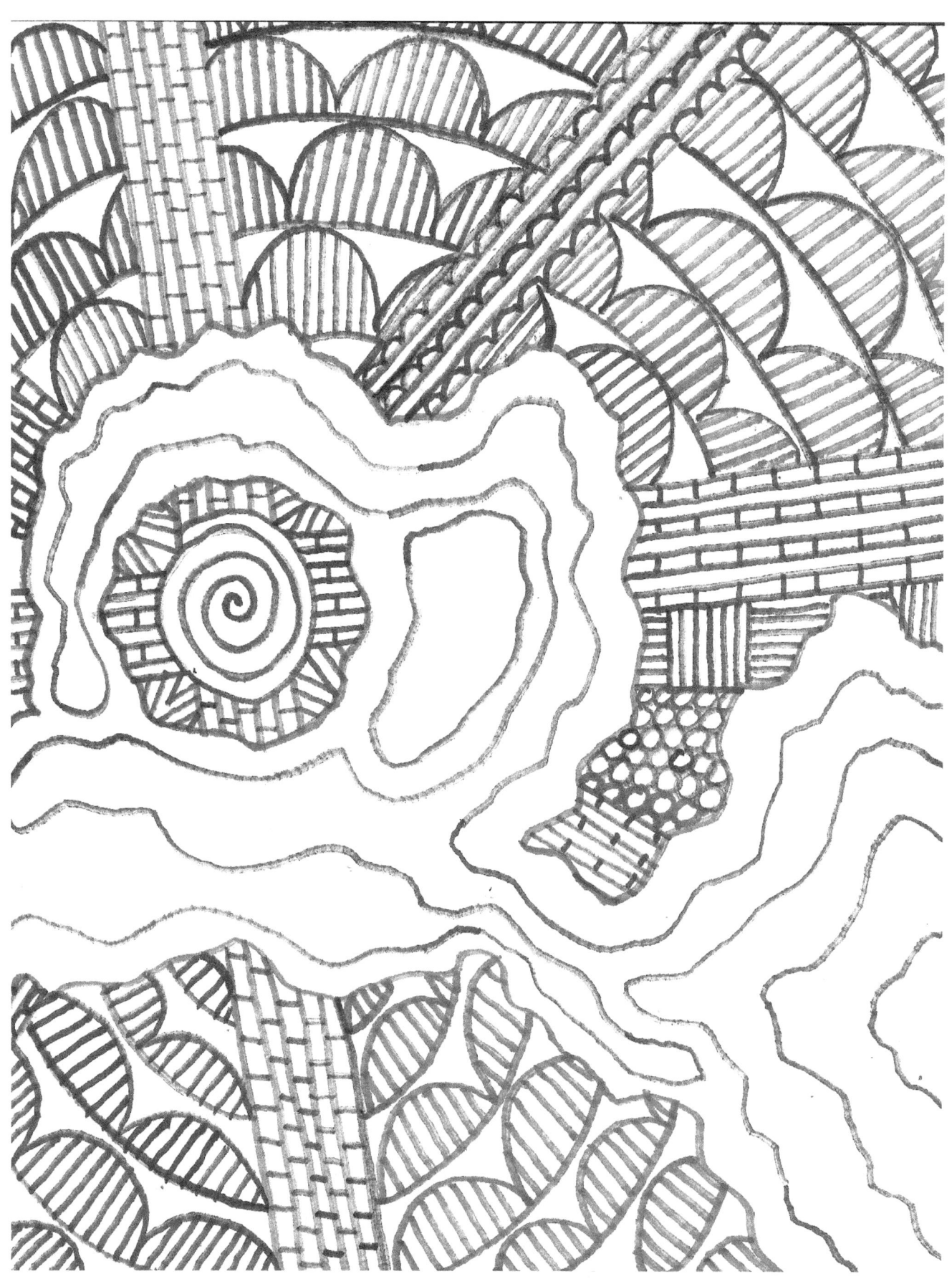

Bobby J. Jones

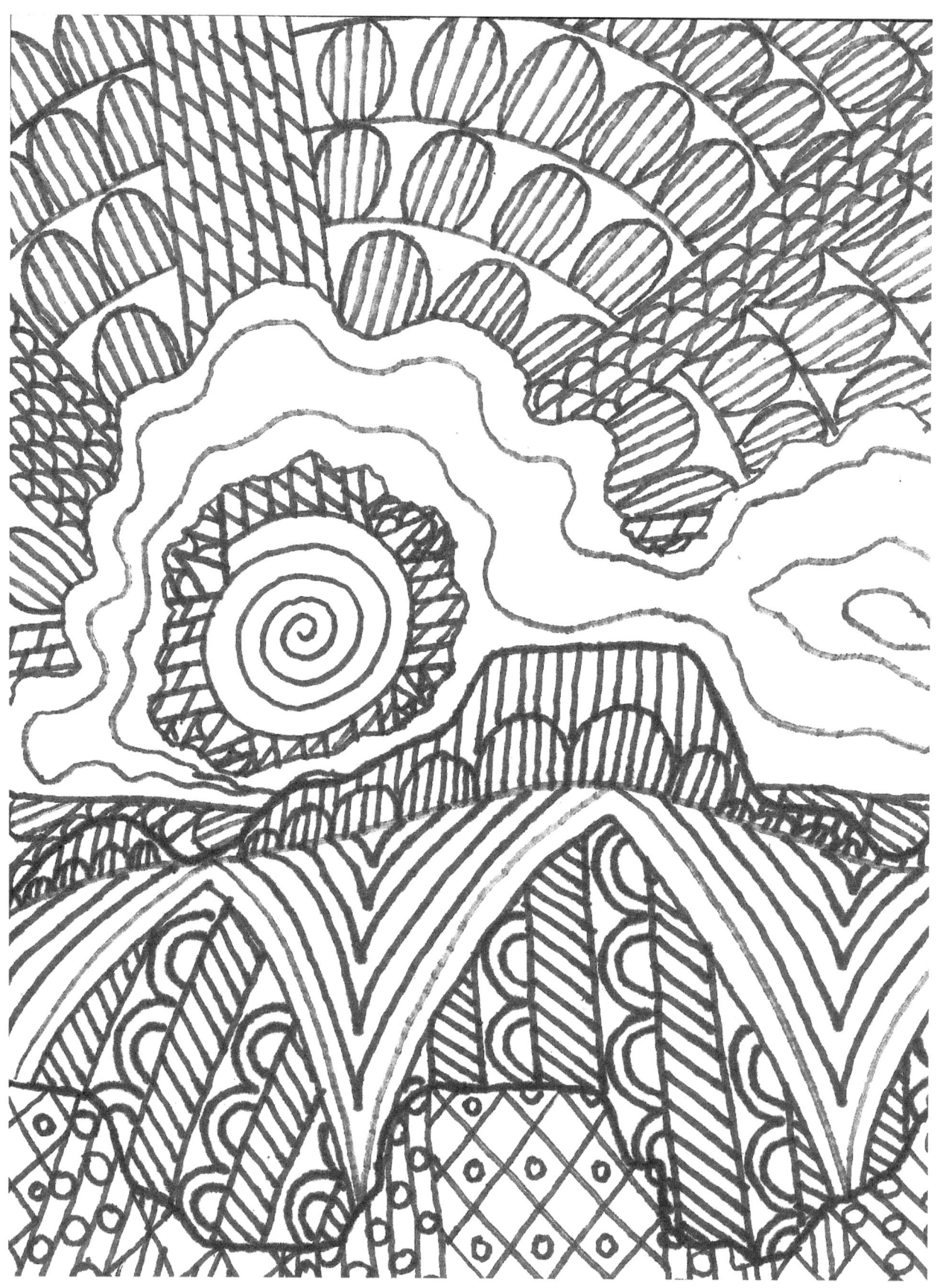

New Mexico Dreamscapes

About The Author

Bobby Jones was born at Reese Air Force Base in Lubbock, Texas in 1966. His family moved to Fort Worth, Texas in 1968. While growing up in Fort Worth, Texas, Jones attended school in The Fort Worth Independent School District. He graduated from Southwest High School in 1985 with honors.

Jones' father Toney Jones worked for General Dynamics as an Industrial Engineer for 25 years while Bobby's mother taught preschool for 20 years at Wedgwood Methodist Church, which became Genesis United Methodist Church in Fort Worth. Jones is the youngest son out of two daughters and two sons. He has two nieces, two nephews, and a great- grandnephew.

Jones attended Texas Tech University in Lubbock, Texas from 1985-1989. He received a BFA in Studio Art (Painting and Drawing) with honors in 1989. Bobby was a member of Alpha Phi Omega at Texas Tech and a member of Golden Key. Then he attended The University of New Mexico in Albuquerque, NM. He obtained a Masters of Art in Art Education (Museum Education, Ceramics, and Photography) in 1994.

Bobby moved to Southern California in 1997 and worked in retail management from 1999 to 2009 for various retail companies in the Palm Springs area. Jones returned to New Mexico in 2009. He worked in the customer service profession from 2010 to 2014.

Jones attended Central New Mexico Community College. Bobby obtained an Alternative Teaching Degree in Special Education and inducted into Phi Theta Kappa. He started working for Albuquerque Public Schools as a substitute teacher in Special Education.

He is currently an Educational Assistant in Special Education in Albuquerque, New Mexico with The Albuquerque Public Schools. Bobby plans to become a teacher in New Mexico. He is also a member of First Unitarian Church in Albuquerque.

Jones is also an artist and creates two dimensional mixed media art that consists of his painting and drawing skills. His artistic inspiration focuses upon the environment of New Mexico. He has exhibited his work at The Factory on 5th, The Tortuga Gallery, The 606 Gallery, and First Unitarian Church's Social Hall.

His artwork appeared in The Desert Sun newspaper (Palm Springs, CA) in the special edition of the first year anniversary of 9/11 and the 40th anniversary of The Kennedy Assassination. Jones also created an art gallery on Facebook, Bobbo66Art Gallery. He invites everyone to look at his art creations.

The artist freehands these original images in this coloring book. Jones does not use computer software programs, rulers or t-squares to create these beautiful images. He enjoys seeing the imperfections in his work. The imperfections are what make Jones' work uniquely original. Jones suggests to the people that buy this book. They can doodle on the blank pages opposite the blackline images or c5reate their own dreamscapes. He is creating a series of coloring books and is creating images for a second coloring book for children of all ages.